Family Math Night 6-8

Host Family Math Nights at your middle school—starting today! Family Math Nights are a great way for teachers to get parents involved in their children's education and to promote math learning outside of the classroom. In this practical book, you'll find step-by-step guidelines and activities to help you bring Family Math Nights to life. The enhanced second edition is aligned with the Common Core State Standards for Mathematical Content and Practice with new activities to help students explain their answers and write about math. It also comes with ready-to-use handouts that you can distribute during your event. With the resources in this book, you'll have everything you need to help students learn essential math concepts—including ratios and proportional relationships, the number system, expressions and equations, geometry, and statistics and probability—in a fun and supportive environment.

Special Features:

- The book is organized by math content, so you can quickly find activities that meet your needs.
- Each activity is easy to implement and includes a page of instructions educators can use to prepare the station, as well as a page for families that explains the activity and can be photocopied and displayed at the station.
- All of the family activities can be photocopied or downloaded from our website, www.routledge.com/9781138200999, so that you can distribute them during your event.

Jennifer Taylor-Cox is owner of Taylor-Cox Instruction, LLC. She serves as an educational consultant for numerous districts across the United States. She teaches university courses in education and is author of 11 Routledge Eye On Education books.

Christine Oberdorf is an administrator with Montgomery County Public Schools in Maryland.

Also Available from Routledge Eye On Education (www.routledge.com/eyeoneducation)

Family Math Night K–5, Second Edition
Common Core State Standards in Action
Jennifer Taylor-Cox

Math Intervention 3–5, Second Edition
Building Number Power with Formative Assessments, Differentiation, and Games
Jennifer Taylor-Cox

Math Intervention PreK–2, Second Edition
Building Number Power with Formative Assessments, Differentiation, and Games
Jennifer Taylor-Cox

Using Formative Assessment to Drive Mathematics Instruction in Grades 3–5
Jennifer Taylor-Cox and Christine Oberdorf

Using Formative Assessment to Drive Mathematics Instruction in Grades PreK–2
Jennifer Taylor-Cox and Christine Oberdorf

Solving Behavior Problems in Math Class
Academic, Learning, Social, and Emotional Empowerment, Grades K–12
Jennifer Taylor-Cox

Family Math Night 6-8

Common Core State Standards in Action

Second Edition

Jennifer Taylor-Cox and Christine Oberdorf

Routledge
Taylor & Francis Group
NEW YORK AND LONDON

Second edition published 2018
by Routledge
605 Third Avenue, New York, NY 10017

and by Routledge
2 Park Square, Milton Park, Abingdon, Oxon, OX14 4RN

Routledge is an imprint of the Taylor & Francis Group, an informa business

© 2018 Taylor & Francis

The right of Jennifer Taylor-Cox and Christine Oberdorf to be identified as authors of this work has been asserted by them in accordance with sections 77 and 78 of the Copyright, Designs and Patents Act 1988.

All rights reserved. No part of this book may be reprinted or reproduced or utilized in any form or by any electronic, mechanical, or other means, now known or hereafter invented, including photocopying and recording, or in any information storage or retrieval system, without permission in writing from the publishers.

Trademark notice: Product or corporate names may be trademarks or registered trademarks, and are used only for identification and explanation without intent to infringe.

First edition published by Eye On Education 2006

Library of Congress Cataloging-in-Publication Data
A catalog record has been requested for this book

ISBN: 978-1-138-20098-2 (hbk)
ISBN: 978-1-138-20099-9 (pbk)
ISBN: 978-1-315-51341-6 (ebk)

Typeset in Times New Roman
by Florence Production Ltd, Stoodleigh, Devon, UK

Art by Maria Diaz Cassi
Visit the eResources at www.routledge.com/9781138200999

Contents

eResources ix
About the Authors x
About Taylor-Cox Instruction xii
About the Illustrator xiii
Acknowledgments xv

Chapter 1: Introduction — 1

    Why Should Our School Have Family Math Night? — 1
    How Is the Book Organized? — 2
    How Are the Activities Connected to the Common Core State Standards? — 3
    Why Should We Use Manipulatives in Mathematics? — 4
    Why Is "Get Students Talking About Math" Included? — 4
    Why Is There a Challenge for Each Activity? — 4
    What Are Some Additional Tips for a Successful Family Math Night? — 5
    What Is the Teacher's Role During Family Math Night? — 6

Chapter 2: Ratios and Proportional Relationships — 7

    Birds Migrating to Florida — 8
    The Tortoise, the Hare, and the Others — 10
    Tweets on Twitter — 12
    Equal Ratios Xs and Os — 14
    Pizza Orders — 16
    Online Shopping — 18

Chapter 3: The Number System — 21

    Baseball Card Collection — 22
    Establishing Order — 24

Lisa's Sub Shop	26
Flip Cup Decimals	28
Target Practice	30
Climb and Slide	32

Chapter 4: Expressions and Equations — 35

Produce Equations	36
Tumble Tower Equivalent Expressions	38
Jeans and Shirts	40
Burning Candles	42
Shoot for the Truth	44
High/Low Takes All	46

Chapter 5: Geometry — 49

Party with Pentominoes	50
Nets Under Construction	52
Chance for Freebies	54
Pythagorean Triples	56
Triangle Cousins	58
Sigmund Transformations	60

Chapter 6: Statistics and Probability — 63

Deep-Sea Diving	64
Lollipops in the Bag	66
Literature Stats	68
The Plot Thickens	70
Texting Tweens	72
Fingerprints	74

Chapter 7: Additional Tools — 77

Family Math Night Invitation to Parents	78
Family Math Night Journal Cover	79

Family Math Night Evaluation	80
Animal Speed Template	81
Tweet Cards	82
Equal Ratios Xs and Os Game Board	83
Online Shopping List	84
Price Adjustment Cards	85
Baseball Card Collection Number Lines	86
Sequence Cards A–I	87
Blank Sequence Cards	88
Lisa's Sub Shop Problem Cards	89
Lisa's Sub Shop Fractions	90
Lisa's Sub Shop Answers	96
Flip Cup Decimals Equation Cards	97
Coordinate Target	98
Rational Number Cards	99
Number Line Mountain	100
Tumble Tower Equivalent Expressions Recording Sheet	101
Tumble Tower Answers	102
Jeans and Shirts Game Board	103
Burning Candles Problem Cards	104
Burning Candles Answers	105
Shoot for the Truth Inequity Cards	106
Shoot for the Truth Inequity Cards Answers	107
High/Low Value Cards	108
Party with Pentominoes Answers	109
Chance for Freebies Place Mat	110
Chance for Freebies Challenge Mat	111
Triangle Cousins Game Board	112
Triangle Cousins Spinner	113
Triangle Cousins Answers	114

Sigmund Transformations Faces	**115**
Sigmund Transformations Game Board	**116**
Sigmund Transformations Key	**117**
Deep-Sea Diving Measures of Center	**118**
Literature Stats Inference Cards	**119**
The Plot Thickens Reference Sheet	**120**
Texting Tweens Problems	**121**
Texting Tweens Answers	**122**
Fingerprint Types Chart	**123**

eResources

All of the family pages in this book are available as free downloads on our website. Visit the eResources at www.routledge.com/9781138200999, so you can easily print and use them during your events.

About the Authors

Dr. Jennifer Taylor-Cox is an energetic, captivating presenter and well-known educator. She is the owner of Taylor-Cox Instruction: Connecting Research and Practice in Education. Jennifer serves as an educational consultant for numerous districts across the United States. Her workshops and keynote speeches are always high-energy and insightful. She earned her Ph.D. from the University of Maryland, and was awarded the "Outstanding Doctoral Research Award" from the University of Maryland and the "Excellence in Teacher Education Award" from Towson University. She currently serves as the president-elect of the Maryland Council of Teachers of Mathematics. Jennifer truly understands how to connect research and practice in education. Her passion for mathematics education is alive in her work with students, parents, teachers, and administrators. Dr. Taylor-Cox lives and has her office in Severna Park, Maryland. She is the mother of three children. If you would like to have Dr. Taylor-Cox present a Family Math Night at your school or if you would like to schedule professional development opportunities for educators and/or parents, please contact her at Taylor-Cox Instruction: Connecting Research and Practice in Education.

Jennifer Taylor-Cox, Ph.D., Educational Consultant
Phone: 410-729-5599
Email: jennifer@taylor-coxinstruction.com

Mrs. Christine Oberdorf is a dedicated and experienced educator. She works as an administrator with Montgomery County Public Schools in Maryland. She earned an M.Ed. from the University of Maryland. As an instructional leader, Chris is committed to teaching children to think and talk like a mathematician and build one's capacity as  a problem-solver and lifelong learner. She seeks opportunities to communicate with teachers and parents to facilitate positive attitudes and meaningful discussion about mathematics.
Mrs. Oberdorf lives in Arnold, Maryland with her husband and two children.

Christine Oberdorf, M.Ed.
Phone: 410-353-1764
Email: christineoberdorf@comcast.net

About Taylor-Cox Instruction

Taylor-Cox Instruction provides professional development for pre-K through grade 12 educators. Jennifer Taylor-Cox and her associates will work with you to design precise and effective professional development opportunities for the educators in your school, district, state, or region. Each professional development opportunity is catered to meet the specific needs of your students, educators, and parents.

Differentiating Math Instruction: Target instruction to meet the learning needs of all students.

Math Intervention: Help struggling ELLs, special needs, and other students find success.

Classroom Discipline: Meet the challenges and help all students succeed.

English Language Learners: Increase content discourse and conceptual understanding for ELL students.

Building Number Power: Bolster all students' number sense and computation.

Family Math Nights: Involve and engage parents and students in learning.

Sigmund Square Finds His Family: With its many geometrical references and humorous storyline, this book offers knowledge and entertainment for learners of all ages! *Published by Taylor-Cox Instruction.*

A free download of the *Sigmund Square Finds His Family* interactive e-book is available at www.routledge.com/9781138200999
To purchase a traditional paperback (ISBN: 978-0-9838880-0-0) or PDF (978-0-9838880-1-7), visit www.SigmundSquare.com

jennifer@taylor-coxinstruction.com · www.taylor-coxinstruction.com · www.sigmundsquare.com

About the Illustrator

It is a pleasure to introduce Maria Diaz Cassi, the illustrator of *Family Math Night 6–8: Common Core State Standards in Action*. I met Maria nearly 30 years ago when she walked into the classroom on the first day of school. I soon learned that she was a smart, creative, compassionate, and determined little first grader. I loved teaching Maria mathematics, reading, writing, science, and social studies. She expressed such a great joy for learning. She loved to draw and doodle. She shared her thoughts of justice and fairness. She advocated for others. It was an honor to be the teacher of such an incredible young lady.

How wonderful it was that we ran into each another a couple of years ago! As a teacher, it is a rare opportunity to see your students much later in their lives. I was not surprised to learn that Maria is still smart, creative, compassionate, and determined. She still believes in justice and serves as advocate for many. Her drawings and doodles have become professional, and I am proud that she created the illustrations for this book.

Our favorite poem in first grade, "Hug O' War" by Shel Silverstein, really describes the world to which we both aspire:

> I will not play at tug o' war.
> I'd rather play at hug o' war,
> Where everyone hugs
> Instead of tugs,
> Where everyone giggles
> And rolls on the rug,
> And everyone kisses,
> And everyone grins,
> And everyone cuddles,
> And everyone wins.

From Maria:

Anytime anyone asks me, "Who was your favorite teacher?" my answer has always been the same, "Dr. Taylor-Cox." She was and still is an amazing teacher. Dr. Taylor-Cox has always been able to make learning fun, rather than burdensome. My memories of being in her classroom, nearly 30 years ago, are filled with smiles and games.

It was a huge honor to work with her and be a part of this project. While working with her, I remembered why I enjoyed being in her class so much. She continues to motivate and spark a desire to learn in others. She is still the same kind, caring, and warm person that she was 30 years ago.

I am so happy that I was able to work with her on this book as the illustrator. It is not every day that you can say that you were not only able to be reunited with your first grade teacher, but able to work on a book with her too!

Acknowledgments

Sincere appreciation is expressed to Joey and Sarah for reviewing the manuscript. Thank you for your acute insight. May you always love math (and each other).

Gratitude is extended to middle school math teacher Bonnie Kellner. Thank you for your expert content knowledge and dedication to mathematics education.

A big shout-out is sent to Ms. Kellner's students at Deep Creek Middle School for providing valuable feedback on the math activities. Thank you for your effective effort and enthusiasm.

The best way to learn math is to do math!

Chapter 1
Introduction

Why Should Our School Have Family Math Night?

The goal of Family Math Night is to strengthen the mathematical aptitudes of students through the power of family interaction. By sponsoring Family Math Night, educators are encouraging parents and students to appreciate the energy and pleasure of mathematics. Each activity is designed to promote mathematical thinking and communication. The hands-on approach presented in this book helps make learning mathematics a meaningful and productive process for all involved.

Parents play an important role in the academic lives of students. By participating in Family Math Night, parents can serve as models of motivation, persistence, and competency to their children. The directions for each activity are presented in a clear, concise manner, allowing parents to guide students to a more complete understanding of various mathematics concepts. At the same time, parents may be acquiring new knowledge and solidifying or revising previous knowledge about mathematics. You may hear parents saying, "I never really understood that concept until I tried this activity," or "I never knew math could be so much fun!" In many ways, the Family Math Night activities enlighten parents as they begin to understand and value mathematics in new ways.

The concepts presented in each Family Math Night activity will help students learn essential new skills and/or reinforce skills already learned in mathematics. While working through math problems in a textbook is one way for some students to learn mathematics, there are other more interactive means of gaining knowledge of mathematics, such as the math stations presented in this book. To help realize a vision of increased math proficiency for all, we need to encourage students to think about and apply mathematics in the real world. Family Math Night can help students and parents become mathematically fulfilled and empowered!

How Is the Book Organized?

Family Math Night Grades 6–8: Common Core State Standards in Action, Second Edition contains seven chapters. The first chapter addresses the goals and intentions of this book. Chapters 2–6 present math stations for five math content domains: ratio and proportional relationships, the number system, expressions and equations, geometry, and statistics and probability. The final chapter provides additional tools for the successful implementation of Family Math Night.

There are two pages for each math station. The first page offers a list of the materials needed for the station, helpful hints, answers, and math standards in action. The second page offers the directions, questions to get students talking about math, and a challenge. The first page is for educators to review and use to prepare each station. The second page can be photocopied and displayed at the Family Math Night station. The directions page can be laminated and mounted. Some educators find it helpful to attach each direction sheet to a file folder. The opened folder can be placed vertically at each station. Other educators prefer to place the direction sheets into display stands or onto display boards. In either case, the point is to have the directions clearly displayed at each station.

How Are the Activities Connected to the Common Core State Standards?

The Common Core State Standards for Mathematics (2010) require a deeper understanding of mathematics. These standards are based on rigorous content, application of knowledge, and alignment with college and career expectations.

The Common Core State Standards for Mathematical Content (2010) define what students should understand. Each Family Math Night station highlights a specific mathematical content domain:

- Ratios and Proportional Relationships (Grades 6–7).
- The Number System (Grades 6–8).
- Expressions and Equations (Grades 6–8).
- Geometry (Kindergarten–Grade 8).
- Statistics and Probability (Grades 6–8).

Note: This book includes activities that build foundations for working with functions (Grade 8), but a specific section is not included.

The Common Core State Standards for Mathematical Practice (2010) describe what students should be doing while engaged in mathematics. Each Family Math Night station highlights two mathematical practices. This is not to imply that these are the only mathematical practices that are connected to the activity. The two mathematical practices listed for each activity were specifically considered during the design of the task and related questions:

- MP1 Make sense of problems and persevere in solving them.
- MP2 Reason abstractly and quantitatively.
- MP3 Construct viable arguments and critique the reasoning of others.
- MP4 Model with mathematics.
- MP5 Use appropriate tools strategically.
- MP6 Attend to precision.
- MP7 Look for and make use of structure.
- MP8 Look for and express regularity in repeated reasoning.

Why Should We Use Manipulatives in Mathematics?

Using manipulatives in mathematics allows students to experience abstract concepts in a concrete manner. Building models to represent mathematical ideas and concepts strengthens the conceptual frameworks students construct as they apply math to everyday life. Manipulatives provide the means by which many students need to express the reasoning and evidence associated with mathematical thinking. Using manipulatives to show how one derives an answer helps solidify understanding. Manipulatives offer students the tools to solve mathematical problems. Additionally, manipulatives often serve as the springboard for mathematical communication as students explain and justify how they solve a problem and/or approach a solution.

To encourage the successful use of math manipulatives, educators should think about how the manipulatives are organized and how they are made available to students. For example, sets of manipulatives can be prepared and stored in plastic bags, baskets, or other containers. The listed manipulatives must be made available to students and parents at each Family Math Night station.

Why Is "Get Students Talking About Math" Included?

Asking questions invites students to engage in mathematical communication. Questions promote mathematical thinking and encourage math discourse. We do not want the Family Math Night room to be a "quiet zone." Instead, we want to strive for a room full of active mathematics participants who are engaged in productive mathematics conversation. By promoting math discourse at Family Math Night, we will better prepare our students for the mathematical challenges ahead. Our role is to provide students with opportunities to hear, use, and come to know the richness of math discourse.

Why Is There a Challenge for Each Activity?

Purposeful challenge serves to inspire and enlighten many students. Each Family Math Night activity includes a challenge that provides a possible extension of the activity. Sometimes students are so engaged in the activity that they want to investigate it further. Other times students go directly to the challenge as a way to increase the level of difficulty. Essentially, the challenges offer a way to differentiate the learning opportunities for students and their families.

What Are Some Additional Tips for a Successful Family Math Night?

If you want high attendance at your Family Math Night, you need to advertise to students and their parents. Send home notices about the event (a sample notice to parents is found on page 78). Include the event in newsletters and on the school calendar. If possible, provide food at the event. Offer incentives for students and parents. Some schools offer recognition to the class with the highest attendance. Other schools encourage students to attend by allowing participation in Family Math Night to serve as the night's homework or serve as extra credit. The possibilities are seemingly endless!

To accommodate many families, you will need a large room or several large rooms. Position the tables and chairs in a manner that allows for maximum movement and comfort. Posting multiple copies of the directions and providing several sets of the materials allow you to have more than one family at each Family Math Night station. If younger siblings are invited, you may want to consider using some of the activities from the elementary-level version of this book, titled *Family Math Night K5: Common Core State Standards in Action*.

Providing a check-in table is a good idea. Parents and students can sign in or teachers can check off students on class lists. The check-in area is a place where students can obtain pencils and Family Math Night journals. The journals can be simple booklets of blank pages for students to record information related to the activities. A sample Family Math Night journal cover is found on page 79. Evaluation forms can also be distributed at the check-in area. A sample Family Math Night evaluation form is found on page 80. The information gathered from the evaluations will help you plan subsequent Family Math Nights.

What Is the Teacher's Role During Family Math Night?

During Family Math Night, educators should facilitate the mathematical endeavors of students and parents. While visiting families at each station, educators should also encourage math dialogue and math thinking. Some of the consumable materials may need to be replenished, and some of the stations need to be monitored. However, be sure to take at least one moment during Family Math Night to notice how the event mathematically inspires and empowers students and parents!

Chapter 2
Ratios and Proportional Relationships

- **Birds Migrating to Florida**
- **The Tortoise, the Hare, and the Others**
- **Tweets on Twitter**
- **Equal Ratios Xs and Os**
- **Pizza Orders**
- **Online Shopping**

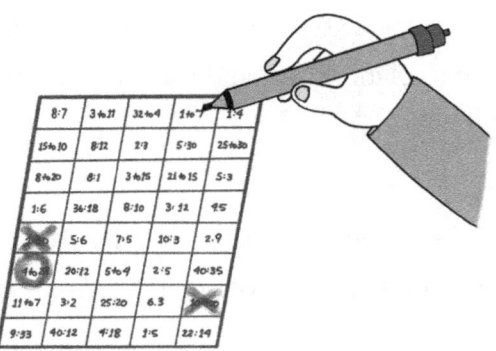

Birds Migrating to Florida

MATERIALS

Receipt tape or strips of paper

HELPFUL HINTS

Display the start of a triple tape diagram. For example:

Days	1	2	3	4
Birds	1	4	7	10
People	1	6	11	16

ANSWERS

28 birds and 46 people will be in Town Square on the tenth day.

43 birds and 71 people will be in Town Square on the fifteenth day.

CHALLENGE ANSWER

To obtain the number of birds on any given day, we need to multiply the number of days (n) by 3 and subtract 2: $3n - 2$.

To obtain the number of people on any given day, we need to multiply the number of days (n) by 5 and subtract 4: $5n - 4$.

COMMON CORE STATE STANDARDS IN ACTION

Math Content: Ratios and Proportional Relationships

- Understand ratio concepts and use ratio reasoning to solve problems.
- Analyze proportional relationships and use them to solve real-world and mathematical problems.

Math Practices

- MP1 Make sense of problems and persevere in solving them.
- MP8 Look for and express regularity in repeated reasoning.

Birds Migrating to Florida

Math Question: Using the given pattern, how many birds and people will be in Town Square on the tenth day?

DIRECTIONS

1. Construct a tape diagram to model the number of days, birds, and people.

> Birds are migrating to Town Square in Fort Lauderdale, Florida. On the first day, 1 bird and 1 person are in Town Square. On the second day, 4 birds and 6 people are in Town Square. On the third day, 7 birds and 11 people are in Town Square. On the fourth day, 10 birds and 16 people are in Town Square. At this rate, how many birds and people will be in Town Square in Fort Lauderdale on the tenth day?

2. Use the information that you know to find out how many birds and people will be in Town Square on the tenth day.

GET STUDENTS TALKING ABOUT MATH

- What pattern(s) do you see?
- What is the relationship between the day and the number of birds and the number of people?
- At this rate, how many birds and people will be in Town Square on the fifteenth day?

★ CHALLENGE

Write an expression that describes the nth term for the relationship between days and birds, and days and people.

Ratios and Proportional Relationships 9

The Tortoise, the Hare, and the Others

MATERIALS

Animal speed template (see page 81)
Yardsticks
Markers
Calculator

HELPFUL HINTS

Have several copies of the animal speed template available.

ANSWERS

Animals in order from slowest to fastest using miles per hour (other units may be applied for comparison):

- Tortoise (0.01 miles per hour)
- Raccoon (12 miles per hour)
- Squirrel (15 miles per hour)
- Chipmunk (21 miles per hour)
- Fox (31 miles per hour)
- Hare (37 miles per hour)

COMMON CORE STATE STANDARDS IN ACTION

Math Content: Ratios and Proportional Relationships

- Understand ratio concepts and use ratio reasoning to solve problems.

Math Practices

- MP2 Reason abstractly and quantitatively.
- MP5 Use appropriate tools strategically.

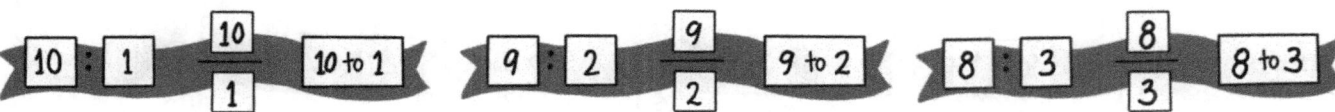

The Tortoise, the Hare, and the Others

Math Question: How do the constant speeds of the animals compare?

DIRECTIONS

1. Review the chart below listing the constant speed of six different animals.
2. Estimate the order of the animals according to speed (slowest to fastest). List and conceal your estimated order.
3. Convert the animal speeds to a common unit and record on the animal speed template.
4. Reveal your estimates and compare with the actual order from slowest to fastest. Determine the player with the most animals in the correct sequence.

Animal	Constant Speed
Tortoise	12 inches per minute
Hare	18.5 miles per half hour
Raccoon	288 miles per day
Chipmunk	1,848 feet per minute
Fox	45.5 feet per second
Squirrel	15 miles per hour

GET STUDENTS TALKING ABOUT MATH

- How do the units compare to one another?
- How did you convert the measurement units using ratio reasoning?
- How did your estimated order compare to the actual order?

★ CHALLENGE

Research the constant speed of another animal and add the animal's rate of speed in the correct location of the sequence.

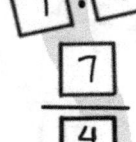

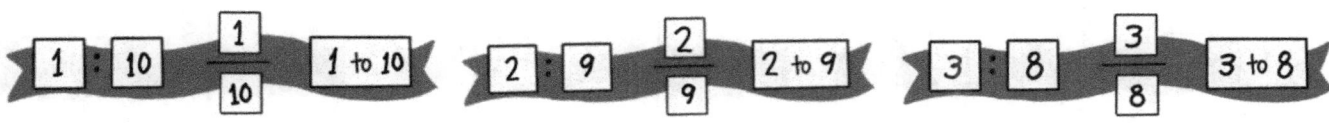

Ratios and Proportional Relationships

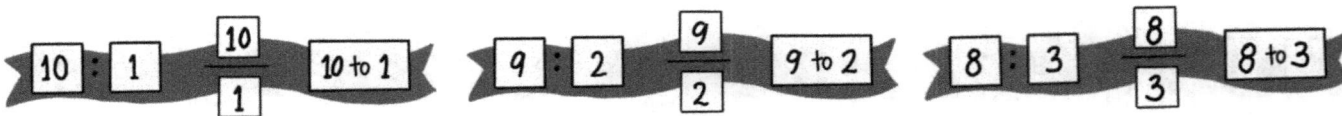

Tweets on Twitter

MATERIALS

Decahedron dice (10-sided, labeled 0–9)

Tweet cards

Paper for tape diagrams

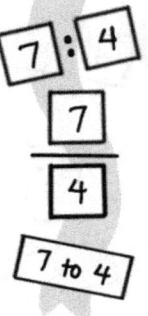

HELPFUL HINTS

Display a model of a tape diagram for participants to use.

Have many copies of the tweet cards available.

ANSWERS

Answers will vary.

COMMON CORE STATE STANDARDS IN ACTION

Math Content: Ratios and Proportional Relationships

- Understand ratio concepts and use ratio reasoning to solve problems.

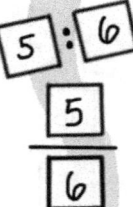

Math Practices

- MP4 Model with mathematics.
- MP8 Look for and express regularity in repeated reasoning.

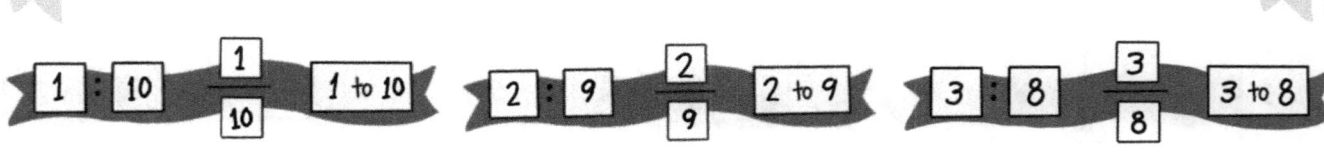

12 *Ratios and Proportional Relationships*

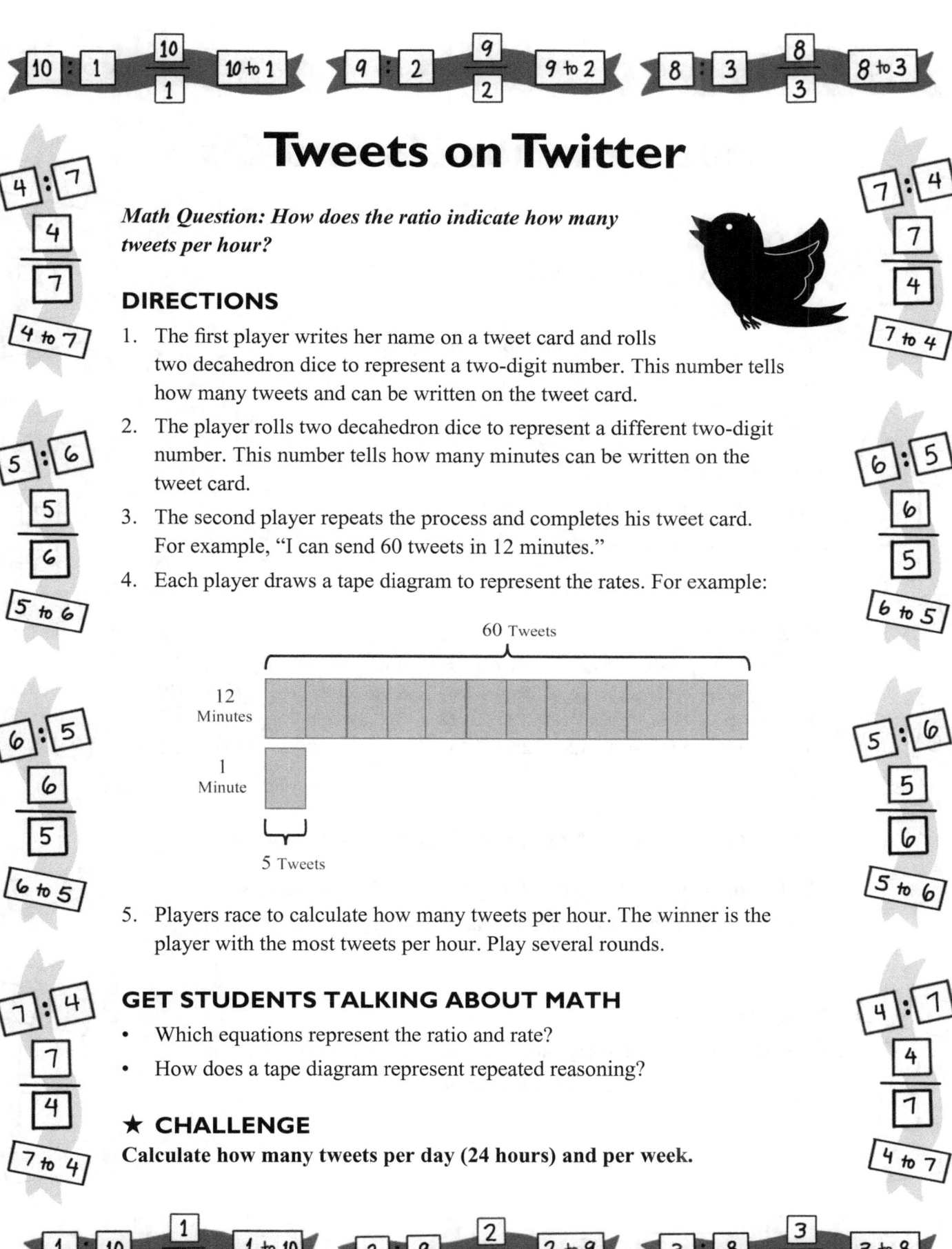

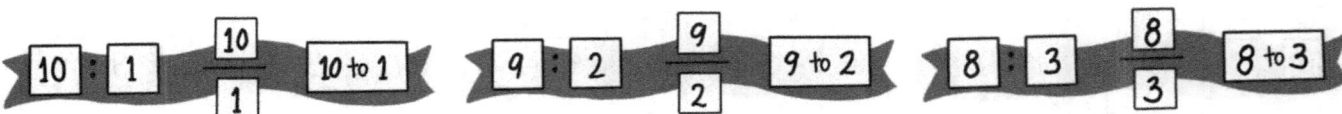

Equal Ratios Xs and Os

MATERIALS

Equal Ratios Xs and Os game board
Timer (30 seconds)
Dry-erase markers (different color for each player)
Erasers

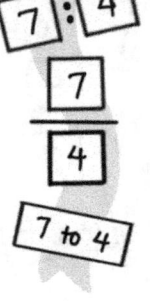

HELPFUL HINTS

Laminate the game boards.
Encourage participants to share their thinking.

ANSWERS

8:7 = 40:35	3 to 11 = 9:33	32 to 4 = 8:1	1 to 7 = 4:28	1:4 = 3:12
15 to 10 = 3:2	8:12 = 2:3	5:30 = 1:6	25 to 30 = 5:6	8 to 20 = 2:5
3 to 15 = 1:5	21 to 15 = 7:5	5:3 = 20:12	36:18 = 6:3	8:10 = 4:5
1:10 = 10:100	5 to 6 = 20 to 24	2:9 = 4:18	10 to 3 = 40:12	11 to 7 = 22:14

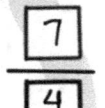

COMMON CORE STATE STANDARDS IN ACTION

Math Content: Ratios and Proportional Relationships

- Understand ratio concepts and use ratio reasoning to solve problems.

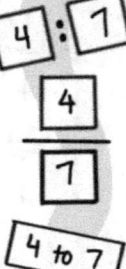

Math Practices

- MP3 Construct viable arguments and critique the reasoning of others.
- MP7 Look for and make use of structure.

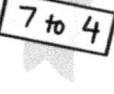
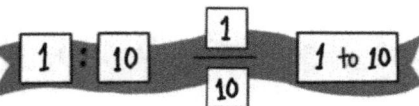

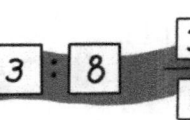
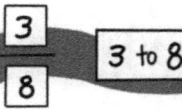

14   *Ratios and Proportional Relationships*

Equal Ratios Xs and Os

Math Question: Which ratios are equivalent?

DIRECTIONS

1. The timer is set and the first player has 30 seconds to find two ratios that are equivalent on the game board. The player marks each ratio with X.

2. The second player has 30 seconds to find two equivalent ratios. The player marks each ratio with O.

3. Players continue taking turns setting the timer for one another and marking equivalent ratios. (*Note*: If equivalent ratios are not found within the allotted time, move to the next player. The allotted time can be modified, if all players agree.)

4. Players should explain their thinking process as the game is played.

5. The winner is the first player to mark four ratios in a row (horizontal, vertical, or diagonal).

GET STUDENTS TALKING ABOUT MATH

- How did you know that the ratios are equivalent?
- What patterns do you notice in the equivalent ratios?

★ CHALLENGE

Try creating your own equivalent ratios or try solving within 15 seconds.

Ratios and Proportional Relationships 15

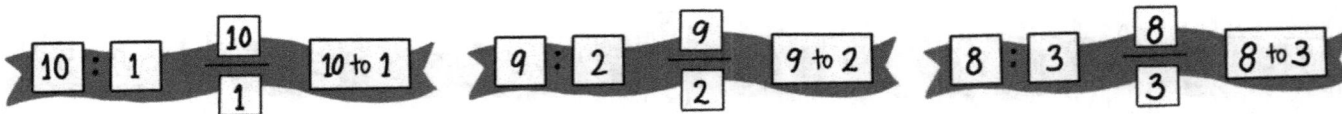

Pizza Orders

MATERIALS

Calculators

HELPFUL HINTS

Encourage students to share their reasoning.

ANSWERS

Answers will vary (see possible representations below).

Class	Ratio of Pizza	Solutions
Freshmen	3 pizzas for every 5 students	$\frac{1}{2} + \frac{1}{10} = \frac{6}{10}$
Sophomores	5 pizzas for every 8 students	$\frac{1}{2} + \frac{1}{8} = \frac{5}{8}$
Juniors	2 pizzas for every 3 students	$\frac{1}{2} + \frac{1}{6} = \frac{4}{6}$
Seniors	7 pizzas for every 10 students	$\frac{1}{2} + \frac{1}{5} = \frac{7}{10}$

Pizzas	7	14	21	28	35	42	49
Students	10	20	30	40	50	60	70

46 pizzas would need to be ordered for 65 seniors.

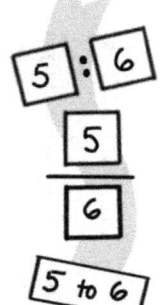

CHALLENGE ANSWERS

$200.00 ÷ $8.99 = 22.25 pizzas

$8.99 × 22 pizzas = $197.78

22 or 11 sets of 2 pizzas were ordered

Each set feeds 3 students

11 × 3 = 33 students

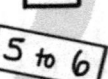

COMMON CORE STATE STANDARDS IN ACTION

Math Content: Ratios and Proportional Relationships

- Analyze proportional relationships and use them to solve real-world and mathematical problems.

Math Practices

- MP1 Make sense of problems and persevere in solving them.
- MP4 Model with mathematics.

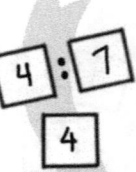

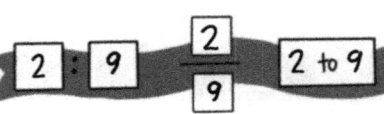
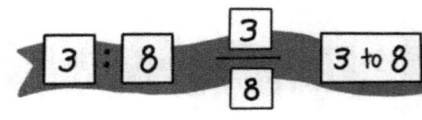

Ratios and Proportional Relationships

Pizza Orders

Math Question: Which class ordered the most pizza per student?

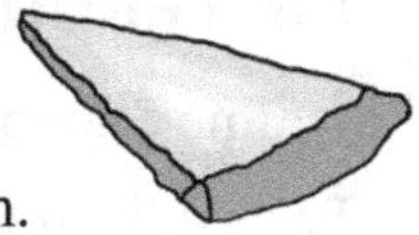

Twin Oaks High School is preparing for homecoming festivities. Students will have pizza as they prepare for the parade competition. Each class used the following ratios to determine how many pizzas to order:

Class	Ratio of Pizza
Freshmen	3 pizzas for every 5 students
Sophomores	5 pizzas for every 8 students
Juniors	2 pizzas for every 3 students
Seniors	7 pizzas for every 10 students

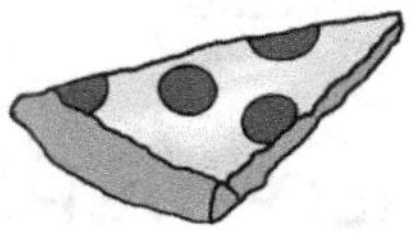

DIRECTIONS

1. Discuss each of the ratios, and estimate which class is providing the most pizza per student.

2. Draw a model to represent the amount of pizza ordered by each class per student. For example, freshmen bought 3 pizzas for every 5 students:

3. If 65 seniors helped, how many pizzas must they order?

 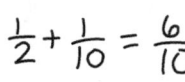

GET STUDENTS TALKING ABOUT MATH

- What strategy did you use to estimate which class ordered the most pizza per student?
- How might you use numbers or pictures to represent the amount of pizza per student for each class?
- Is there a significant difference in the amount of pizza ordered per student by each class? Why or why not?

★ CHALLENGE

If each pizza costs $8.99 and the junior class spent just under $200.00 for pizza, how many students from the junior class helped with homecoming preparations? How do you know?

Ratios and Proportional Relationships 17

Online Shopping

MATERIALS

Online Shopping list (see page 84)
Price adjustment cards (see page 85)
Digital device with Internet access
Calculator

HELPFUL HINTS

Provide multiple copies of the Online Shopping list and several sets of the price adjustment cards.

Many students carry cell phones, which may be utilized for this task. Consider providing computers, tablets, or Chromebooks for students requiring access to a device.

ANSWERS

Answers will vary based on items selected for online purchase.

CHALLENGE ANSWERS

Answers will vary based on items selected for online purchase.

COMMON CORE STATE STANDARDS IN ACTION

Math Content: Ratios and Proportional Relationships

- Analyze proportional relationships and use them to solve real-world and mathematical problems.

Math Practices

- MP1 Make sense of problems and persevere in solving them.
- MP6 Attend to precision.

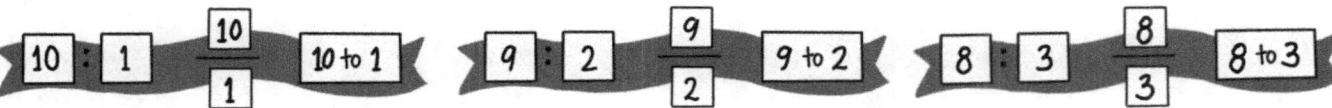

Online Shopping

Math Question: What will be the final cost for each item?

DIRECTIONS

1. Each shopper lists five items he wishes to purchase on the Online Shopping list (see sample table below).
2. Use the Internet to shop for each item. Compare the price on more than one site before recording the best purchase price.
3. Randomly draw five price adjustment cards.
4. Using the same five cards, each shopper decides which price adjustment card to pair with each item on his list to result in the greatest savings.
5. Calculate the final cost of each item with the price adjustment.
6. Determine which shopper saved the most money when applying the price adjustments. For example:

Item	List Price	Price Adjustment	Final Price
1. Backpack	$55.95	−$5.00	$50.95
2. Sneakers	$99.99		
3. Bike	$175.95		
4. Movie	$15.99		
5.			

GET STUDENTS TALKING ABOUT MATH

- What is your estimated cost for all five items?
- How will the price adjustment affect the final cost?
- For which item will the adjustment have the greatest impact? How do you know?

★ CHALLENGE

Calculate the highest possible price you would have paid for the items on your list based on the price adjustment cards selected.

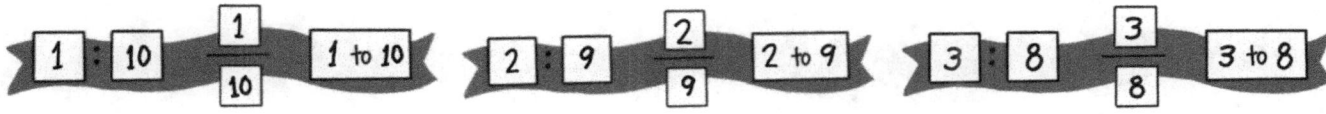

Ratios and Proportional Relationships 19

Chapter 3
The Number System

- **Baseball Card Collection**
- **Establishing Order**
- **Lisa's Sub Shop**
- **Flip Cup Decimals**
- **Target Practice**
- **Climb and Slide**

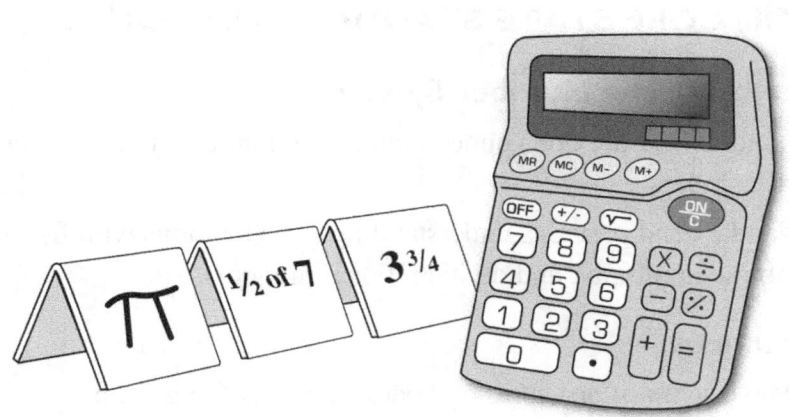

Baseball Card Collection

MATERIALS

Pretend money ($100 bills) or Base Ten Blocks (100 flats) or Digi-Blocks (100 blocks)

Baseball cards (or index cards to represent the collection)

Baseball Card Collection number lines (see page 86), laminated full page of number lines for each player

Dry-erase markers and erasers

HELPFUL HINTS

Keeping track of how much money Marvin and Leon spend and earn helps participants accurately solve this problem. Additionally, it is important for participants to clarify how much money with which Leon and Marvin began.

ANSWERS

Marvin made $200.00, Leon lost $200.00

CHALLENGE ANSWERS

Marvin made $500.00, Leon lost $500.00

COMMON CORE STATE STANDARDS IN ACTION

Math Content: The Number System

- Apply and extend previous understandings of numbers to the system of rational numbers.
- Apply and extend previous understandings of operations with fractions to add, subtract, multiply, and divide rational numbers.

Math Practices

- MP1 Make sense of problems and persevere in solving them.
- MP4 Model with mathematics.

Baseball Card Collection

Math Question: How much money, if any, do Marvin or Leon make or lose?

DIRECTIONS

1. To role-play this math situation, decide who will be Marvin and who will be Leon.
2. Gather supplies to represent money and the baseball card collection. Role-play the math situation.

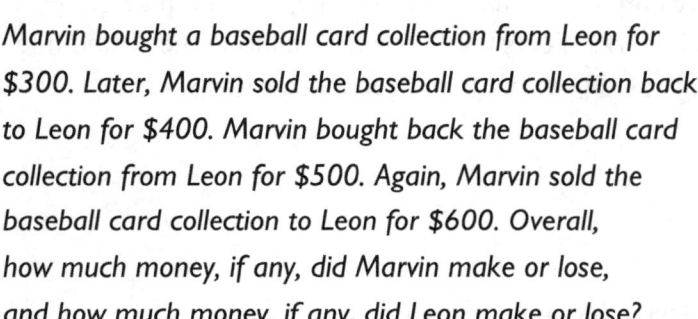

> Marvin bought a baseball card collection from Leon for $300. Later, Marvin sold the baseball card collection back to Leon for $400. Marvin bought back the baseball card collection from Leon for $500. Again, Marvin sold the baseball card collection to Leon for $600. Overall, how much money, if any, did Marvin make or lose, and how much money, if any, did Leon make or lose?

3. Represent each transaction on a number line diagram.

GET STUDENTS TALKING ABOUT MATH

- Does the answer make sense?
- How does the number line diagram help model the math?
- Does it matter how much money Marvin or Leon has in the beginning? Why or why not?

★ CHALLENGE

If the pattern continues, how much money, if any, will Marvin make or lose after he buys back *and* sells for the fifth time? What about Leon?

The Number System 23

Establishing Order

MATERIALS

Sequence cards A–I (see page 87)

Blank sequence cards (see page 88)

Calculators

HELPFUL HINTS

Provide several sets of the sequence cards.

Copy sets of the sequence cards on different colored paper to help keep the sets organized (card stock works nicely). Fold each card along the dotted line to create a standing tent. Provide several blank sequence cards for the challenge.

ANSWERS

The sequence from smallest value to largest value is:

I G F H B D C E A

COMMON CORE STATE STANDARDS IN ACTION

Math Content: The Number System

- Compute fluently with multi-digit numbers.

Math Practices

- MP2 Reason abstractly and quantitatively.
- MP6 Attend to precision.

Establishing Order

Math Question: What is the value for each card?

DIRECTIONS

1. Read each sequence card and estimate the value. Write estimates in your math journal.
2. Place the cards in order from least to greatest based on your estimates.
3. Verify your sequence by calculating the answer for each sequence card.
4. Adjust your sequence as necessary.

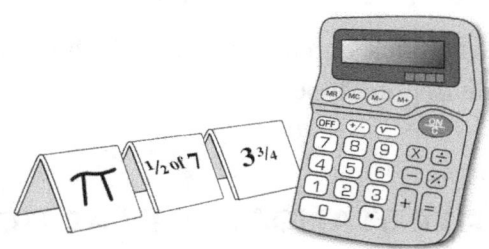

GET STUDENTS TALKING ABOUT MATH

- What strategy did you use to find your estimate?
- How did your estimated sequence compare to the actual sequence? Between which two sequence cards is the smallest difference?
- What is the advantage of estimating before calculating?

★ CHALLENGE

Create a new sequence card and determine where it belongs in the sequence.

Lisa's Sub Shop

MATERIALS

Lisa's Sub Shop problem cards (see page 89)

Lisa's Sub Shop fractions (see page 90)

Lisa's Sub Shop answers (see page 96)

Dry-erase markers and erasers

Fraction bars or other fraction manipulatives

HELPFUL HINTS

Copy sub fractions on card stock, cut apart, and laminate.

Using a different color of card stock for each type of sub shop fraction can help students easily recognize the fraction types.

COMMON CORE STATE STANDARDS IN ACTION

Math Content: The Number System

- Apply and extend previous understandings of multiplication and division to divide fractions by fractions.

Math Practices

- MP1 Make sense of problems and persevere in solving them.
- MP2 Reason abstractly and quantitatively.

Lisa's Sub Shop

Math Question: How can we represent the division of fractions?

DIRECTIONS

1. Shuffle problem cards and place face down in a pile.
2. Arrange sub fractions face up on the table.
   (*Note*: Players can use fraction bars or other manipulatives as representations.)
3. The first player chooses a problem card, writes the equation, and locates the corresponding sub fractions. For example: How many $\frac{1}{3}$ servings can you get out of $\frac{1}{2}$ of a sub?

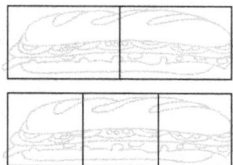
$\frac{1}{2} \div \frac{1}{3}$

4. Shade $\frac{1}{2}$ of the sub fraction that is divided into halves. Shade the same amount of the sub fraction (serving) that is divided into thirds.

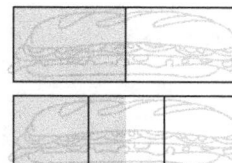
$\frac{1}{2} \div \frac{1}{3} = 1\frac{1}{2}$

5. Solve. The quotient serves as the player's score.
6. Players take turns solving the problem cards with the sub fraction models. Players keep a running total. The winner is the first player to reach 10 or more.

GET STUDENTS TALKING ABOUT MATH

- How do you know how many servings?
- How does your understanding of division of whole numbers help you with the division of fractions?

★ CHALLENGE
Try sketching fraction bars to represent the sub fractions.

Flip Cup Decimals

MATERIALS

Set of 10 plastic cups (labeled 0–9 on bottom and inside of cup) for each player

Flip Cup Decimals equation cards (see page 97)

Calculators

HELPFUL HINTS

Use a thick permanent marker to write the digits on the cups (one digit 0–9 on the bottom and inside of each cup makes one set).

This activity needs enough room for each participant to line up a set of cups on the edge of the table.

ANSWERS

A. 1   B. 8   C. 5   D. 2   E. 3   F. 9   G. 7   H. 8   I. 4   J. 6   K. 6
L. 0   M. 1   N. 4   O. 5   P. 3

COMMON CORE STATE STANDARDS IN ACTION

Math Content: The Number System

- Compute fluently with multi-digit numbers and find common factors and multiples.

Math Practices

- MP2 Reason abstractly and quantitatively.
- MP6 Attend to precision.

Flip Cup Decimals

Math Question: Which digit is needed to complete the decimal equation?

DIRECTIONS

1. Each player lines up one set of cups (0–9) face up on the edge of the table with part of each cup hanging off the edge.
2. Each player draws one random decimals equation card.
3. Each player examines the equation to find the missing digit.
4. Players race to flip the cup of the missing digit. (*Note*: Use one finger to flip the cup so that it lands face down. If the cup does not land face down, reposition the cup on the edge of the table and try again.)

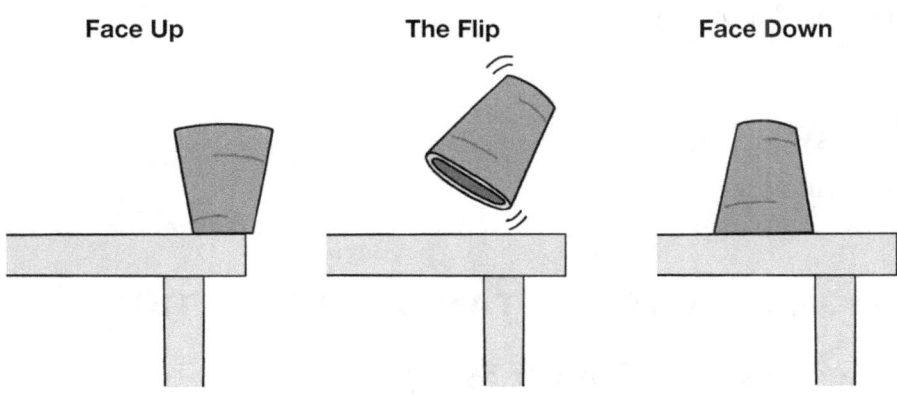

| Face Up | The Flip | Face Down |

5. The first player to flip the correct missing digit cup to the face down position scores 10 points.
6. Players check solutions with calculators.
7. Play continues until a player scores 50 points.

GET STUDENTS TALKING ABOUT MATH

- How did you find the missing digit?
- Is there a more efficient way to find the missing digit?

★ CHALLENGE
Try creating problems with missing digits for other players to solve.

Target Practice

MATERIALS

Coordinate target (see page 98), laminated

Tape

Meter stick

Cotton swabs

Colored chalk

Paper towels and wet wipes

HELPFUL HINTS

Copy the coordinate target on card stock.

Tape the coordinate target to the wall or to a box.

ANSWERS

Answers will vary.

COMMON CORE STATE STANDARDS IN ACTION

Math Content: The Number System

- Apply and extend previous understandings to the system of rational numbers.

Math Practices

- MP6 Attend to precision.
- MP7 Look for and make use of structure.

Target Practice

Math Question: How are the coordinates related?

DIRECTIONS

1. The first player colors one side of a cotton swab with chalk and names the predicted quadrant (I, II, III, IV) and coordinates (*x*, *y*).

2. The first player stands/sits about one meter from the target and tosses the cotton swab at the coordinate target.

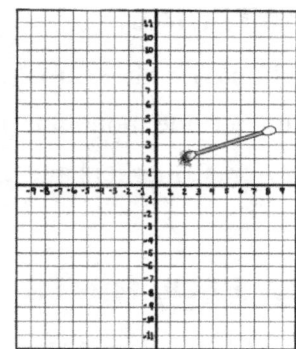

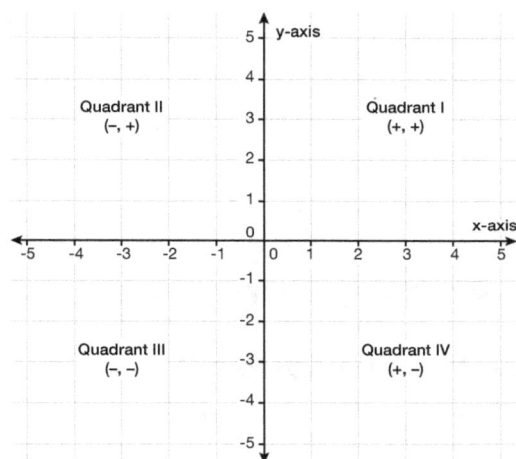

3. The player earns 10 points for predicting the correct quadrant, 100 points for predicting the correct *x* axis, 100 points for predicting the correct *y* axis, and 1,000 points for correctly predicting both coordinates.

4. Players take turns. The winner is the player with the most points after five rounds.

GET STUDENTS TALKING ABOUT MATH

- How far away is your chalk spot from your predicted coordinates?
- What patterns do you notice about the coordinate grid?

★ CHALLENGE

Try tossing two cotton swabs at the same time (remember to make your prediction).

The Number System 31

Climb and Slide

MATERIALS

Rational number cards (see page 99)

Number line mountain (see page 100) for each player, laminated

Dry-erase markers and erasers

HELPFUL HINTS

Copy rational number cards on card stock. Make each set a different color for easy sorting.

ANSWERS

Answers will vary.

COMMON CORE STATE STANDARDS IN ACTION

Math Content: The Number System

- Apply and extend previous understandings of numbers to the system of rational numbers.
- Apply and extend previous understandings of operations with fractions to add, subtract, multiply, and divide rational numbers.

Math Practices

- MP3 Construct viable arguments and critique the reasoning of others.
- MP4 Model with mathematics.

Climb and Slide

Math Question: How can you determine the absolute value?

DIRECTIONS

1. Each player is dealt four number cards (face down).
2. Players flip over one card at a time and use the marker to represent the journey on the mountain number line. Positive numbers are units climbed up, and negative numbers are units slid back down.

   For example:
   $+ 5 - 2 + 4 - 3$

3. Players find the value of the journey (final location on the mountain number line) by adding climbs and subtracting slides $(+ 5 - 2 + 4 - 3 = 4)$.
4. Players find the absolute value of the journey (combining each part of the journey) by adding climbs and slides $(+ 5 - 2 + 4 - 3 = 4)$.
5. Players compare values. The player with the highest absolute value wins the round.
6. Play continues until a player wins five or more rounds.

GET STUDENTS TALKING ABOUT MATH

- What is the relationship between value and absolute value?
- What are some ways to represent adding and subtracting rational numbers?

★ CHALLENGE
Try using five or more number cards.

The Number System 33

Chapter 4
Expressions and Equations

- **Produce Equations**
- **Tumble Tower Equivalent Expressions**
- **Jeans and Shirts**
- **Burning Candles**
- **Shoot for the Truth**
- **High/Low Takes All**

Produce Equations

MATERIALS

Snap cubes (yellow, orange, and red)

HELPFUL HINTS

The snap cubes enable participants to simulate substitution. The specific colors represent the three fruit types.

ANSWERS

One grapefruit and two apples do *not* equal three pears.

Given	$3p = 4a$
Given	$1g = 2a + 1p$
What you are looking for	$1g + 2a \stackrel{?}{=} 3p$
Substitute	$2a + 1p$ for $1g$
From second given equation	$2a + 1p + 2a \stackrel{?}{=} 3p$
Combine $2a + 2a$	$4a + 1p \stackrel{?}{=} 3p$
Substitute	$3p$ for $4a$
From first given equation	$3p + 1p \stackrel{?}{=} 3p$
Combine $3p + 1p$	$4p \neq 3p$

One way to rewrite the quantities to make them equal: one grapefruit + two apples – one pear = three pears

COMMON CORE STATE STANDARDS IN ACTION

Math Content: Expressions and Equations

- Solve real-life mathematical problems using numerical and algebraic expressions and equations.

Math Practices

- MP1 Make sense of problems and persevere in solving them.
- MP3 Construct viable arguments and critique the reasoning of others.

Produce Equations

Math Question: Are the given quantities equal?

> *If three pears weigh the same as four apples*
>
> *and*
>
> *one grapefruit weighs the same as two apples and one pear,*
>
> *will*
>
> *one grapefruit and two apples weigh the same as three pears?*

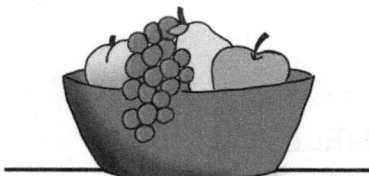

DIRECTIONS
1. Read the question above and use the snap cubes to model the problem.
2. Decide whether the equation "one grapefruit and two apples weigh the same as three pears" is true.
3. If you think the equation is true, explain why. If you think the equation is not true, rewrite it to make it true.

GET STUDENTS TALKING ABOUT MATH
- How might the snap cubes help to solve this problem?
- How do the fruit values compare to one another? How do you know?

★ CHALLENGE
Write additional equations using apples, pears, and grapefruit in your math journal.

Expressions and Equations

Tumble Tower Equivalent Expressions

MATERIALS

54 Tumble Tower blocks (Jenga blocks)

Tumble Tower Equivalent Expressions recording sheets (see page 101), multiple copies

HELPFUL HINTS

Label the 54 blocks ahead of time: two blocks for each letter A–Z and two blocks with AA. Label one of the large rectangle faces so that the label cannot be read until the block is removed from the tower.

Have many copies of the recording sheet available.

Place answers in an envelope marked "answers" to allow participants to check their solutions.

ANSWERS

See page 102.

COMMON CORE STATE STANDARDS IN ACTION

Math Content: Expressions and Equations

- Apply and extend previous understandings of arithmetic to algebraic expressions.

Math Practices

- MP1 Make sense of problems and persevere in solving them.
- MP8 Look for and express regularity in repeated reasoning.

Tumble Tower Equivalent Expressions

Math Question: How are algebraic expressions distributed and simplified?

DIRECTIONS

1. Players build the tower by stacking the blocks in sets of three. The blocks in each layer should be perpendicular to the previous layer. The letters are randomly placed and the tower is straightened before the game begins.

2. The first player carefully takes one block out from any layer except for the top two complete layers. The player can push or pull the block, but can only use one hand.

3. Once the block is removed, the player reads the letter and finds the equivalent expression on his recording sheet.

4. The player writes the missing initial expression, distributed expression, or simplified expression on his recording sheet.

5. The player places the block on top of the tower (following the layered pattern).

6. Players take turns removing blocks and writing equivalent expressions until the tower falls.

7. Players check answers. One point is earned for each correct answer. The player who made the tower fall subtracts three points from his score. The winner is the player with the highest score.

GET STUDENTS TALKING ABOUT MATH

- How will you use what is known to write an equivalent expression?
- Do the repeated calculations offer any generalizations? If so, what are they?

★ CHALLENGE
Try adding two expressions to distribute and simplify.

Expressions and Equations

Jeans and Shirts

MATERIALS

Jeans and Shirts game board for each player (see page 103)

Dry-erase markers and erasers

Die (six-sided, labeled 1–6)

Paper, pencils, and paper clips

HELPFUL HINTS

Copy the game boards on card stock and laminate.

To use the spinner, set a paper clip on the spinner.

Place a pencil point through one end of the paper clip at the center of the spinner. Holding the pencil securely with one hand, spin the paper clip with the other hand.

ANSWERS

Answers will vary.

COMMON CORE STATE STANDARDS IN ACTION

Math Content: Expressions and Equations

- Apply and extend previous understandings of arithmetic to algebraic expressions.
- Reason about and solve one-variable equations and inequalities.

Math Practices

- MP3 Construct viable arguments and critique the reasoning of others.
- MP6 Attend to precision.

Jeans and Shirts

Math Question: Which algebraic expression is least?

DIRECTIONS

1. The first player rolls one die. All players write the number as "how many?" jeans.

2. The next player rolls the die. All players write the number as "how many?" shirts. (*Note*: Each player uses her own game board. The numbers rolled are shared by all players, but each player spins her own values (use a paper clip and pencil to create the spinner.)

3. Each player spins the spinner (at the same time) to find out the cost (of each) and then spins to find out the discount (off the total) for the jeans and then the shirts.

4. Players record the equation that represents the total cost:

   (number of jeans × jeans cost) − jeans discount = jeans total

   For example, 2 jeans that cost $50 with $10 discount plus

   3 shirts that cost $25 each with a $19 discount is recorded

   (2 × $50) − $10 + (3 × $25) − $19 = $146

5. The player with the least cost is the winner of the round!

6. Play several rounds.

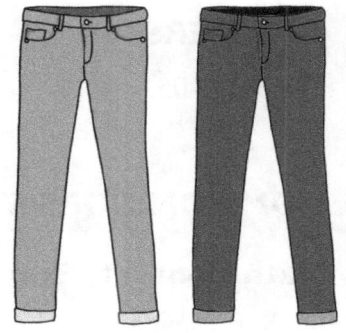

GET STUDENTS TALKING ABOUT MATH

- How could you test your approach to solving the problem?
- Are the parentheses important in this problem? Why or why not?

★ CHALLENGE
Try including pairs of shoes or hats, or try rolling two dice.

Burning Candles

MATERIALS

Burning Candles problem cards (see page 104)

Graph paper

Pencils

HELPFUL HINTS

Copy problem cards on card stock, cut out, and laminate.

Place answers in an envelope for participants to check for accuracy.

ANSWERS

See page 105.

COMMON CORE STATE STANDARDS IN ACTION

Math Content: Expressions and Equations

- Represent and analyze quantitative relationships between dependent and independent variables.

Math Practices

- MP5 Use appropriate tools strategically.
- MP8 Look for and express regularity in repeated reasoning.

Burning Candles

Math Question: What is the relationship between the hours burning and the height of the candle?

DIRECTIONS

1. Shuffle problem cards and place in a pile, face down.
2. Each player takes one card from the pile.
3. Players create a table to represent the height y of the candle after burning x hours.
4. After the tables are complete, players switch tables and race to graph the linear relationship.
5. The winner is the first player to complete the graph with all necessary components.

Graph

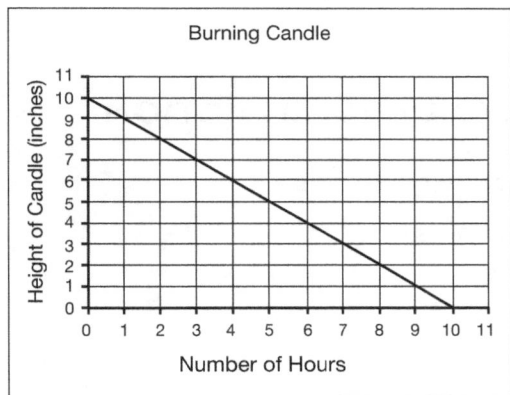

Table

| Burning Candle ||
Number of hours candle burns (x)	Height of candle in inches (y)
0	10
1	9
2	8
3	7
4	6
5	5
6	4
7	3
8	2
9	1
10	0

GET STUDENTS TALKING ABOUT MATH

- What is the initial height of the candle?
- How would you describe the slope?

★ CHALLENGE

Try writing the linear equations.

height of candle = rate at which it burns × number of hours burned + initial height

$y = -1 \times x + 10$, or $y = 10 - x$

Expressions and Equations

Shoot for the Truth

MATERIALS

Shoot for the Truth inequity cards for each player (see page 106)

Three large cups or three small bowls, one labeled with the > symbol, one labeled with the < symbol, and one labeled with the = symbol

Timer

HELPFUL HINTS

Label cups or bowls on both sides with a permanent marker. Each player needs a set of inequity cards in a unique color. The cards are not reusable.

ANSWERS

See page 107.

COMMON CORE STATE STANDARDS IN ACTION

Math Content: Expressions and Equations
- Work with radicals and integer exponents.

Math Practices
- MP6 Attend to precision.
- MP7 Look for and make use of structure.

Shoot for the Truth

Math Question: Which sign makes the sentence true?

DIRECTIONS

1. Each player receives a set of inequity cards in a unique color.

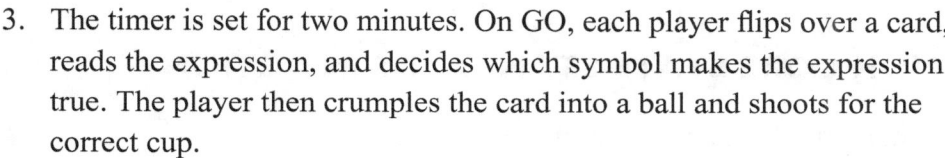

2. Players are positioned on each side of the table with the three cups in the center and equal distance from all players (or teams if more than two or three players).

3. The timer is set for two minutes. On GO, each player flips over a card, reads the expression, and decides which symbol makes the expression true. The player then crumples the card into a ball and shoots for the correct cup.

4. When time expires, each cup is checked to ensure the expressions are matched with the correct sign. Players receive a point for each expression of unique color in the correct cup. Players lose two points for each incorrect match.

5. The player with the highest total from all three cups is the winner.

GET STUDENTS TALKING ABOUT MATH

- How does the power of 10 impact the value?
- What do you notice about the exponent and the effect on the value?

★ CHALLENGE
Describe your strategy to make a quick and accurate decision.

High/Low Takes All

MATERIALS

High/low value cards (see page 108)

HELPFUL HINTS

Copy several sets of the value cards on card stock. Make each set a different color for easy sorting.

ANSWERS

Answers will vary.

COMMON CORE STATE STANDARDS IN ACTION

Math Content: Expressions and Equations

- Work with radicals and integer exponents.

Math Practices

- MP3 Construct viable arguments and critique the reasoning of others.
- MP6 Attend to precision.

High/Low Takes All

Math Question: How do the values compare to one another?

DIRECTIONS

1. Shuffle the cards and distribute equally among two to four players.
2. Players decide if the winner is the player with the highest value or the player with the lowest value.
3. Each player flips over one card. All players compare the value of each card and determine the winner of the round. If the values are equal, each player flips a second card to compare.
4. The winner collects all cards from the round.
5. Play continues until a player has no remaining cards.
6. The player with the most cards wins.

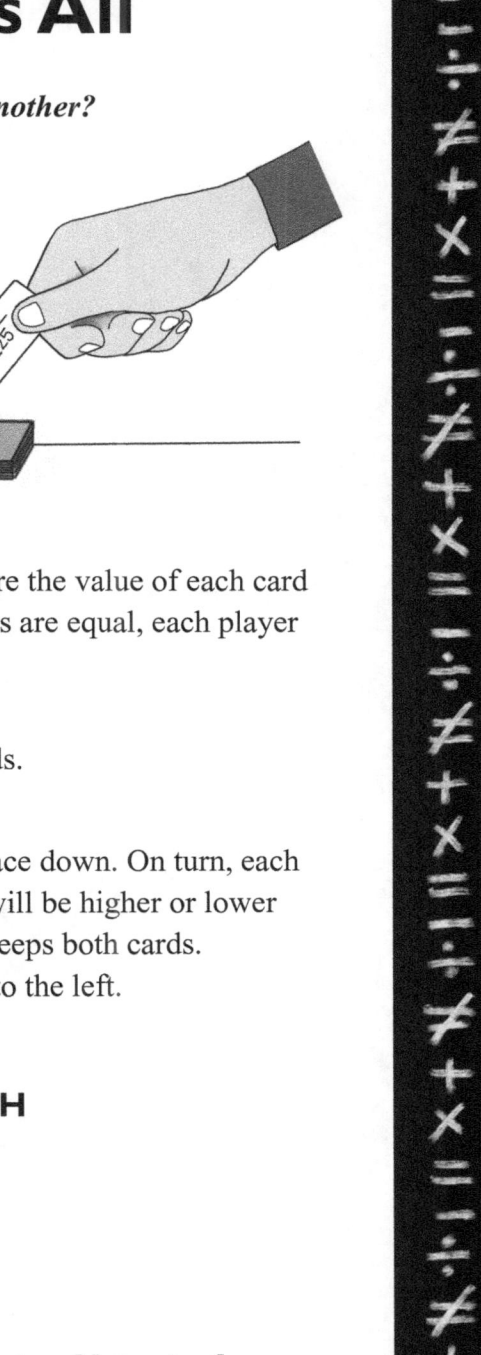

Variation: Shuffle all cards and place in a single pile face down. On turn, each player flips a card and predicts whether the next card will be higher or lower before flipping the second card. If correct, the player keeps both cards. If incorrect, the player passes both cards to the player to the left.

GET STUDENTS TALKING ABOUT MATH

- Which card has the greatest/least value?
- What strategy did you use to find the value?

★ CHALLENGE
Mentally calculate the difference between the highest and lowest value.

Expressions and Equations

Chapter 5
Geometry

- Party with Pentominoes
- Nets Under Construction
- Chance for Freebies
- Pythagorean Triples
- Triangle Cousins
- Sigmund Transformations

Party with Pentominoes

MATERIALS

Square tiles

Graph paper

Scissors

Answer key (see page 109) in folder or envelope

HELPFUL HINTS

Display at least one of the pentominoes as an example.

Place the answer key in a folder or envelope labeled "Answers" so that participants try creating several different pentominoes before looking at answers.

ANSWERS

See page 109.

COMMON CORE STATE STANDARDS IN ACTION

Math Content: Geometry

- Solve real-world and mathematical problems involving area, surface area, and volume.

Math Practices

- MP6 Attend to precision.
- MP7 Look for and make use of structure.

Party with Pentominoes

Math Questions: How can the squares be arranged to make 12 different pentominoes? How can the pentominoes be arranged to form a rectangle?

DIRECTIONS

1. Make a pentomino by grouping five squares together so that every square has at least one of its sides in common with at least one other square.

2. One example of a pentomino is a rectangle formed by lining up all five squares. Try making more complex pentominoes (such as a "T" form). There are 12 different pentominoes. (*Note*: If the pentominoes are congruent—same shape flipped or rotated— they are not considered different.)

3. Draw your pentominoes on graph paper and cut them out.

4. Try using all 12 pentominoes to construct a 6×10 rectangle.

GET STUDENTS TALKING ABOUT MATH

- How do you know that you have made a different pentomino?
- Do all of the pentominoes have the same area? Do all of the pentominoes have the same perimeter?
- Which pentominoes can be folded to make a cube without a lid?

★ CHALLENGE

Try using all 12 pentominoes to construct a 5×12 rectangle or a 4×15 rectangle or a 3×20 rectangle.

Nets Under Construction

MATERIALS

Geometric solids

Tag board

Scissors

Rulers

Compass

Clear tape

HELPFUL HINTS

The geometric solids provided should include, but not be limited to, cylinders, triangular pyramids, rectangular pyramids, triangular prisms, rectangular prisms (including cubes), and cones.

ANSWERS

Solutions will vary based on the choice of geometric solids. The task is self-correcting because students may compare the two solids for congruency.

COMMON CORE STATE STANDARDS IN ACTION

Math Content: Geometry

- Solve real-world and mathematical problems involving area, surface area, and volume.

Math Practices

- MP4 Model with mathematics.
- MP5 Use appropriate tools strategically.

Nets Under Construction

Math Question: What does the 2D net look like for a 3D figure?

DIRECTIONS

1. Choose from the collection of geometric solids.
2. Draw a net on the tag board for the solid, using the actual solid as a measurement and tracing tool. For example:

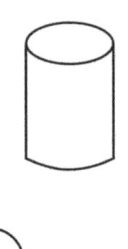

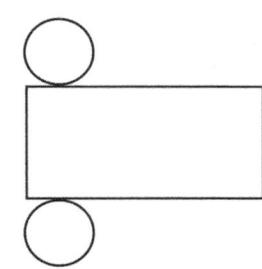

3. Cut out the tracing to create the net.
4. Fold and assemble the net to create a solid congruent to the original.
5. Calculate surface area and volume.

GET STUDENTS TALKING ABOUT MATH

- What are the shapes of the face, bases, and/or surfaces of the solid?
- If the volume was doubled, how would the surface area change?
- Could a different net be created and folded to create the same solid?

★ CHALLENGE

Determine the dimensions of volume of a solid with twice the surface area of the original solid.

Chance for Freebies

MATERIALS

Calculators

Rulers

Compasses

Place mat (see page 110)

Challenge mat (see page 111)

HELPFUL HINTS

Provide copies of the challenge mat. The challenge mat can be photocopied on the back of the place mat page.

ANSWERS

Area of the mat: 8.5 in. × 6.25 in. = 53.125 in.^{2}

Probability of winning = area of shape ÷ area of mat

Dessert   2 in.^{2} ÷ 53.125 in.^{2} = .038 = 3.8%

Beverage   1.77 in.^{2} ÷ 52.125 in.^{2} = .033 = 3.3%

Salad   1.5 in.^{2} ÷ 53.125 in.^{2} = .028 = 2.8%

Meal   4.91 in.^{2} ÷ 53.125 in.^{2} = .092 = 9.2%

Probability of winning = area of all shapes ÷ area of mat

Anything   2 in.^{2} + 1.77 in.^{2} + 1.5 in.^{2} + 4.91 in.^{2} = 10.18 in.^{2}

   10.18 in.^{2} ÷ 53.125 in.^{2} = .192 = 19.2%

   or

   .038 + .033 + .028 + .092 = .191 = 19.1%

COMMON CORE STATE STANDARDS IN ACTION

Math Content: Geometry

- Solve real-world and mathematical problems involving area, surface area, and volume.

Math Practices

- MP1 Make sense of problems and persevere in solving them.
- MP5 Use appropriate tools strategically.

Chance for Freebies

Math Question: What is the probability of winning a free item?

A local restaurant provides a special offer at the conclusion of each meal in an attempt to boost business. The waitperson drops a dinner mint onto the place mat of each customer. If the mint lands on any part of the designated figures, the charge for that item is subtracted from the bill.

Note: For this simulation, do not consider the size of the mint.

DIRECTIONS

1. Look at the place mat and calculate the probability of a customer receiving each item for free. Base your answer on the dimensions of the mat, 8.5 in. × 6.25 in.
2. Calculate the probability of a customer receiving any item for free.
3. Discuss whether this is a beneficial practice for the restaurant owner.

GET STUDENTS TALKING ABOUT MATH

- What do you estimate the probability to be?
- Which item do you have the greatest chance of receiving for free? How do you know?
- How does the area of a rectangle relate to the area of a triangle?

★ CHALLENGE
Sketch a new mat with about a 30% chance of winning a free menu item.

Pythagorean Triples

MATERIALS

Centimeter grid paper

Centimeter cubes

HELPFUL HINTS

The grid paper and cubes provide a hands-on approach for representing $a^2 + b^2 = c^2$.

ANSWERS

3, 4, **5**

5, 12, **13**

6, 8, **10**

8, 15, **17**

12, 16, **20**

CHALLENGE ANSWERS

7, 24, **25**

This is one of many possible answers.

COMMON CORE STATE STANDARDS IN ACTION

Math Content: Geometry

- Understand and apply the Pythagorean theorem.

Math Practices

- MP4 Model with mathematics.
- MP8 Look for and express regularity in repeated reasoning.

Pythagorean Triples

Math Question: What is the third value in the Pythagorean triples?

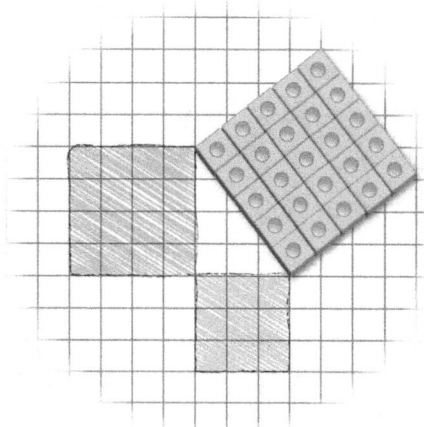

DIRECTIONS

1. Draw a right angle on the grid paper with one side 3 cm long and the other side 4 cm long (see the figure to the right).
2. Sketch the square for each of the two sides.
3. Draw the hypotenuse (diagonal) to form a triangle.
4. Using a 5×5 array of centimeter cubes, create the square for the hypotenuse. Place this array on the hypotenuse and compare the area of the hypotenuse square with the sum of the areas of the squares of the legs.
5. Complete the following Pythagorean triples:

    5, 12, ?   6, 8, ?   8, 15, ?   12, 16, ?

GET STUDENTS TALKING ABOUT MATH

- What relationship do you notice among the areas of the squares?
- How many Pythagorean triples do you think there are? Why?

★ CHALLENGE
Find the missing lengths in this Pythagorean triple: ___, 24, ___.

Triangle Cousins

MATERIALS

Sigmund Square Finds His Family by Jennifer Taylor-Cox

Angle viewers or protractors

Triangle Cousins game board (see page 112), laminated

Triangle Cousins spinner (see page 113), paper clips

Dry-erase markers and erasers

Paper and pencils for drawing angles

HELPFUL HINTS

The e-book version of *Sigmund Square Finds His Family* can be downloaded at www.routledge.com/9781138200999 and used on a laptop, desktop, Promethean, or smart board. Note the interactive features.

Copy the chart/spinner on card stock and laminate.

To use the spinner, set a paper clip on the spinner.

Place a pencil point through one end of the paper clip at the center of the spinner. Holding the pencil securely with one hand, spin the paper clip with the other hand.

ANSWERS

See page 114.

CHALLENGE ANSWERS

See page 114.

COMMON CORE STATE STANDARDS IN ACTION

Math Content: Geometry

- Solve real-world and mathematical problems involving angle measure, area, surface area, and volume.

Math Practices

- MP5 Use appropriate tools strategically.
- MP8 Look for and express regularity in repeated reasoning.

58   *Geometry*

Triangle Cousins

Math Question: How do we identify the size of the interior angles of a triangle?

DIRECTIONS

1. Read *Sigmund Square Finds His Family* by Jennifer Taylor-Cox. Review page 7 and look for different triangles throughout the book.
2. Each player uses a Triangle Cousins game board and spinner.
3. The first player spins the angle spinner. If this angle measurement accurately fits in one of the blank spots on the chart, the player draws the angle and writes that angle measurement on the chart.
4. The second player repeats the process using her chart. (*Note*: If the measurement does not accurately fit in one of the blank spaces on the chart, the player loses her turn. If a player decides that she would like to erase a previously placed angle measurement, she must skip a spin to do so.)
5. The winner is the first player to accurately complete her Triangle Cousins game board.

GET STUDENTS TALKING ABOUT MATH

- Which tools are helpful? Why?
- How are different types of triangles alike or different?

★ CHALLENGE
How is the sum of the interior angles of a triangle related to the sum of the interior angles of a rectangle? A pentagon?

Sigmund Transformations

MATERIALS

Sigmund Square Finds His Family by Jennifer Taylor-Cox

Sigmund Transformations faces (see page 115), one per player

Sigmund Transformations game board (see page 116), one per player

Sigmund Transformations key (see page 117)

Geo-reflectors (also called Miras) and dice

HELPFUL HINTS

The e-book version of *Sigmund Square Finds His Family* can be downloaded at www.sigmundsquare.com and used on a laptop, desktop, Promethean, Chromebook, or smart board. Note the interactive features.

Cut out two Sigmund profiles and tape them back to back in a manner that represents Sigmund's reflection when flipped over.

ANSWERS

Answers will vary.

COMMON CORE STATE STANDARDS IN ACTION

Math Content: Geometry

- Draw, construct, and describe geometrical figures and describe the relationships between them.
- Understand congruence and similarity using physical models, transparencies, or geometry software.

Math Practices

- MP3 Construct viable arguments and critique the reasoning of others.
- MP7 Look for and make use of structure.

Sigmund Transformations

Math Question: What do transformations look like?

DIRECTIONS

1. Read *Sigmund Square Finds His Family* by Jennifer Taylor-Cox. Review page 16.
2. Talk about flips, slides, and turns. In this activity:

   Flip is the reflection of a figure.

   Slide is the figure positioned (translated) one unit away.

   Turn is the figure rotated one unit (a 90-degree turn).

3. Each player uses his own Sigmund face and game board.
4. Place Sigmund's face in the start position. Take turns spinning the spinner to find out if Sigmund will flip, slide, or turn. Players may choose the transformation on "Choice."
5. Roll the dice to find out how many transformations. Each transformation is based on the previous.
6. Use the geo-reflector to record Sigmund's position by drawing his face in the square after each move.
7. The winner is the first player to get Sigmund "home."

GET STUDENTS TALKING ABOUT MATH

- How will you represent the transformation?
- Which transformation is the most complex?
- How many turns equal a slide or flip?

★ CHALLENGE
Try drawing dilations of Sigmund.

Chapter 6
Statistics and Probability

- **Deep-Sea Diving**
- **Lollipops in the Bag**
- **Literature Stats**
- **The Plot Thickens**
- **Texting Tweens**
- **Fingerprints**

Deep-Sea Diving

MATERIALS

Bag of gems or cubes or other counters

Calculators

Mean, median, mode, and range definitions (see page 118)

HELPFUL HINTS

Glass gems can often be purchased at the dollar store or craft store.

Post definitions of mean, median, mode, and range.

ANSWERS

An example set of data is provided; however, students' data sets will vary based on size of hand and size of gems.

12, 13, 14, 14, 14, 15, 15, 17, 18, 18

Mean = 15

Median = 14.5

Mode = 14

Range = 6

500 ÷ 15   = 33.33, which would require 34 dives

500 ÷ 14.5 = 34.48, which would require 35 dives

500 ÷ 14   = 35.71, which would require 36 dives

COMMON CORE STATE STANDARDS IN ACTION

Math Content: Statistics and Probability

- Develop an understanding of statistical variability.
- Summarize and describe distributions.

Math Practices

- MP2 Reason abstractly and quantitatively.
- MP6 Attend to precision.

Deep-Sea Diving

Math Question: How many handfuls will it take to retrieve 500 gems?

DIRECTIONS

1. Use the bag of gems (or cubes) to find the average amount that can be retrieved with one handful. Reach in the bag, get a handful, and then count the gems. Record the number of gems in the handful in your math journal. Place the gems back in the bag and repeat the process nine more times.

As a deep-sea diver, you just discovered a treasure chest that is firmly attached to the ocean floor. The gems can be removed, but only one handful at a time. You have 10 practice dives to find out how many dives it will take you to recover 500 gems.

2. Record the number of gems retrieved in each of the 10 handfuls. Find the mean, median, mode, and range of the set of data that you collected. Using this information, discuss how many dives are needed to retrieve 500 gems.

GET STUDENTS TALKING ABOUT MATH

- How many gems do you think you will get in the next handful? Why?
- Which measure of center best describes those data? Why?
- How many dives do you think it would take to retrieve 1,500 gems? How do you know?

★ CHALLENGE
Try the experiment using two hands to collect gems.

Lollipops in the Bag

MATERIALS

2 Paper bags

Red and yellow objects to represent lollipops

HELPFUL HINTS

Many people inaccurately think the answer to this problem is $\frac{1}{2}$.

The key to finding the correct answer is understanding that there are four possible outcomes: red + red, red + yellow, yellow + red, and yellow + yellow. Three out of the four outcomes include at least one red lollipop.

ANSWERS

$\frac{3}{4}$ or 3 out of 4 or $\frac{12}{16}$ or 75%

A sample tree diagram is provided; however, student work may vary.

The first bag contains R1 R2 Y1 Y2.

The second bag contains R3 R4 Y3 Y4.

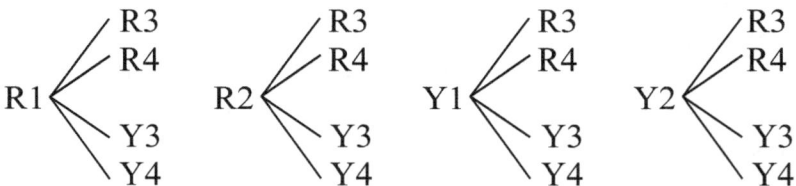

COMMON CORE STATE STANDARDS IN ACTION

Math Content: Statistics and Probability

- Investigate chance processes and develop, use, and evaluate probability models.

Math Practices

- MP3 Construct viable arguments and critique the reasoning of others.
- MP4 Model with mathematics.

Lollipops in the Bag

Math Question: What is the chance of getting at least one red lollipop?

DIRECTIONS

1. Create a tree diagram, table, or organized list to determine the probability.

Each bag contains two red lollipops and two yellow lollipops (four lollipops per bag—a total of eight lollipops). If you reach in the bags (without looking) and take out one lollipop from each, what are the chances that you will get at least one red lollipop?

2. Explain the strategy you used to solve this problem.

GET STUDENTS TALKING ABOUT MATH

- How can you organize all of the possible outcomes?
- What are the chances of getting zero red lollipops?
- How many ways can you get at least one red lollipop? How do you know the answer is not 1 out of 2?

★ CHALLENGE
Try creating your own "lollipop scenario" involving probability.

Statistics and Probability

Literature Stats

MATERIALS

Literature Stats inference cards (see page 119)

Three or more copies of several print materials (books, magazines, online articles, poems, etc.)

Calculators

HELPFUL HINTS

It may be beneficial to offer this activity in the media center for easy access to a variety of print resources.

ANSWERS

Answers will vary based on print materials selected.

CHALLENGE ANSWERS

Answers will vary based on print materials selected.

COMMON CORE STATE STANDARDS IN ACTION

Math Content: Statistics and Probability

- Draw informal comparative inferences about two populations.

Math Practices

- MP3 Construct viable arguments and critique the reasoning of others.
- MP6 Attend to precision.

Literature Stats

Math Question: What statistical comparisons may you infer about literature?

DIRECTIONS

1. Players (up to three) agree on which literature title to select for the activity.

2. Each player uses data gathered through random sampling to draw inferences about each piece and records on the Literature Stats inference card:
   - median number of words per line;
   - mean number of lines per page or stanza; and
   - average word length in entire piece.

3. Each player describes his inferences and methodology with the other players. Collectively, all players discuss and critique the inferences, and identify the most precise inference based on the methodology used.

GET STUDENTS TALKING ABOUT MATH

- How is each measure of center impacted by the sample size?
- How large should the sample size be to make a reasonable inference?
- How might you justify your methodology?
- What is the variance among the inferences? What accounts for the differences?

★ CHALLENGE

Draw inferences about a second piece of literature and compare the statistics from the two populations (literature sources).

The Plot Thickens

MATERIALS

Chart-size graph paper
Markers
Calculators
The Plot Thickens reference sheet (see page 120)

ANSWERS

Line Plot:

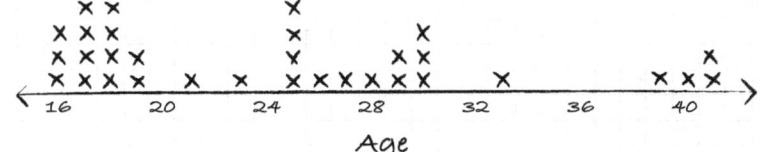

Histogram:

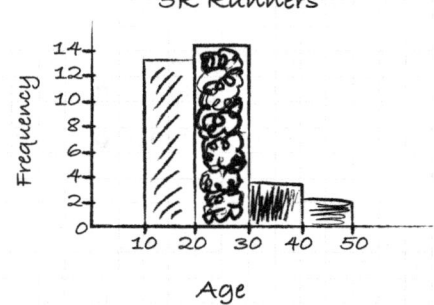

Box Plot:

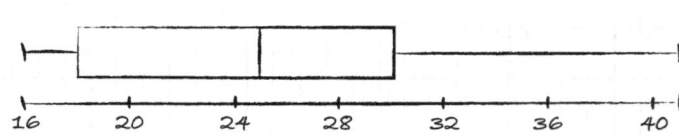

COMMON CORE STATE STANDARDS IN ACTION

Math Content: Statistics and Probability

- Summarize and describe distributions.

Math Practices

- MP4 Model with mathematics.
- MP6 Attend to precision.

70 *Statistics and Probability*

The Plot Thickens

Math Question: What do various plot displays reveal about a data set?

The softball team at Broadway High School recently hosted a 5K run to benefit the local children's hospital. The school would like to analyze the data to identify the target audience for future planning and advertising.

DIRECTIONS

1. Review the data set showing the age of the participants who ran in the 5K race (also provided on the reference sheet).

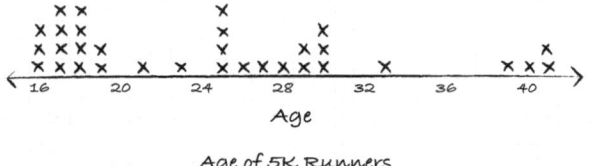
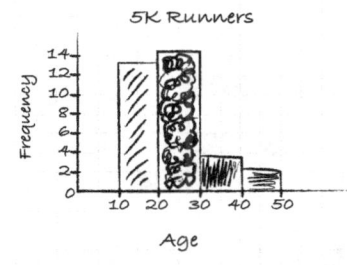
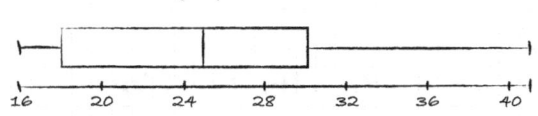

2. Create a poster to display the data set on a line plot, a histogram, and a box plot. Use the reference sheet as a model.
3. Label the target audience on the poster, and list some implications for future planning.

GET STUDENTS TALKING ABOUT MATH

- What can you see on the line plot that is not as visible on the histogram?
- What might a box plot show more readily than a histogram or line plot?
- Without the data set, would you be able to find the median age from each display? Why or why not?

★ CHALLENGE
Consider and discuss whether all displays illustrate the variability in the age distribution. Explain your thinking.

Texting Tweens

MATERIALS

Texting Tweens problems (see page 121)

Texting Tweens answers (see page 122)

Timer

HELPFUL HINTS

Copy problem cards on one color of card stock.

Copy answer cards on a different color of card stock.

Label the back of each card with the corresponding letter.

ANSWERS

See page 122.

COMMON CORE STATE STANDARDS IN ACTION

Math Content: Statistics and Probability
- Summarize and describe distributions.
- Draw informal comparative data inferences about two populations.

Math Practices
- MP1 Make sense of problems and persevere in solving them.
- MP6 Attend to precision.

Texting Tweens

Math Question: How can you describe the data distributions in a box plot?

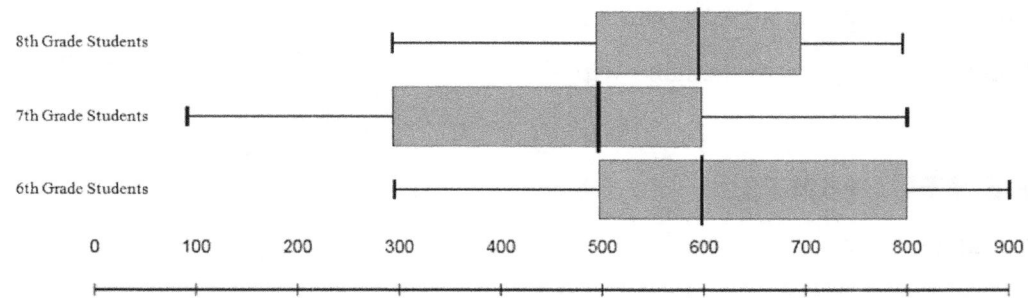

Text Messages Sent by Students at LOL Middle School per Month

DIRECTIONS

1. The first player chooses a problem and starts the timer.
2. When the first person answers the question, the second player stops the timer.
3. The second player checks the corresponding answer and scores the player:
   - Correct answer in 30 seconds or less +2
   - Correct answer in more than 30 seconds +1
   - Incorrect answer in more than 30 seconds −1
   - Incorrect answer in 30 seconds or less −2
4. Players take turns and keep a running score. The winner is the first player to score 7 points or more.

GET STUDENTS TALKING ABOUT MATH
- What do you notice about how the data are distributed?
- How would you explain box plots?

★ CHALLENGE
Discuss how the data may look different for elementary students.

Statistics and Probability 73

Fingerprints

MATERIALS

Ink pad, paper, magnifying glasses/hand lenses/magnifiers

Index cards

Fingerprint types chart (see page 123)

Calculators, paper towels, hand wipes

HELPFUL HINTS

Laminate fingerprint types chart

ANSWERS

In this data set, there is an association between:

"Whorl" fingerprint type and >$50,000 annual salary

"Loop" fingerprint type and $20,000–50,000 annual salary

"Arch" fingerprint type and <$20,000 annual salary

"Loop" fingerprint type is the most common

COMMON CORE STATE STANDARDS IN ACTION

Math Content: Statistics and Probability

- Investigate patterns of association in bivariate data.

Math Practices

- MP1 Make sense of problems and persevere in solving them.
- MP4 Model with mathematics.

Fingerprints

Math Question: How can we calculate the relative frequencies to see if there is an association in bivariate categorical data?

DIRECTIONS

1. Use the ink pad to make your fingerprint.
2. Use the fingerprint types chart to identify your fingerprint type.
3. Investigate the pattern of association in bivariate categorical data. Consider fingerprint type and annual income.
4. Interpret the two-way table summarizing data collected on 25-year-olds working in Washington, DC.

	Arch		Whorl		Loop		Total	
	Male	Female	Male	Female	Male	Female	Male	Female
<$20,000	856	912	241	263	1,401	1,327	2,498	2,502
$20,000–50,000	1,805	1,755	763	694	2,439	2,544	5,007	4,993
>$50,000	321	298	912	1,077	1,277	1,115	2,510	2,490

5. Calculate the appropriate relative frequencies. Describe the pattern of association.

GET STUDENTS TALKING ABOUT MATH

- Which fingerprint type is most common?
- Is there an association between annual salary and fingerprint type? Explain.
- Is there an association between gender and fingerprint type? Explain.

★ CHALLENGE

Discuss how the chart could be displayed if additional data, such as where each person lives, were collected.

Statistics and Probability

Chapter 7
Additional Tools

- Family Math Night Invitation to Parents
- Family Math Night Journal Cover
- Family Math Night Evaluation
- Animal Speed Template
- Tweet Cards
- Equal Ratios Xs and Os Game Board
- Online Shopping List
- Price Adjustment Cards
- Baseball Card Collection Number Lines
- Sequence Cards A–I
- Blank Sequence Cards
- Lisa's Sub Shop Problem Cards
- Lisa's Sub Shop Fractions
- Lisa's Sub Shop Answers
- Flip Cup Decimals Equation Cards
- Coordinate Target
- Rational Number Cards
- Number Line Mountain
- Tumble Tower Equivalent Expressions Recording Sheet
- Tumble Tower Answers
- Jeans and Shirts Game Board
- Burning Candles Problem Cards
- Burning Candles Answers
- Shoot for the Truth Inequity Cards
- Shoot for the Truth Inequity Cards Answers
- High/Low Value Cards
- Party with Pentominoes Answers
- Chance for Freebies Place Mat
- Chance for Freebies Challenge Mat
- Triangle Cousins Game Board
- Triangle Cousins Spinner
- Triangle Cousins Answers
- Sigmund Transformations Faces
- Sigmund Transformations Game Board
- Sigmund Transformations Key
- Deep-Sea Diving Measures of Center
- Literature Stats Inference Cards
- The Plot Thickens Reference Sheet
- Texting Tweens Problems
- Texting Tweens Answers
- Fingerprint Types Chart

Family Math Night Invitation to Parents

On

_____ (date and time),

_____ (school name)

will hold an exciting event called **Family Math Night!**

Students, parents, siblings, and other relatives are invited to attend a fun-filled evening of mathematical pleasure. The intent of **Family Math Night** is to participate in math standards in action as we strengthen the mathematical application, problem solving, and communication skills of students through the power of family interaction.

We encourage you to continue to support your child's mathematical growth through your participation in Family Math Night.

Family Math Night Journal Cover

Family Math Night at _____
                                                    School Name

_____
                 Date

Family Math Night:
Middle School Math Standards in Action
MATH JOURNAL

Student's Name: _____

Family Math Night Evaluation

_____
School Name

Date _____

Did you enjoy the Family Math Night?	
Which activity did you like the best?	
Which activity do you plan to try again at home?	
Would you change anything about Family Math Night?	

Signed (Student) _____

Signed (Parent/Guest) _____

Date _____

ANIMAL SPEED TEMPLATE

Animal	Constant Speed	Common Unit Speed
Tortoise	12 inches per minute	
Hare	18.5 miles per half hour	
Raccoon	288 miles per day	
Chipmunk	1,848 feet per minute	
Fox	45.5 feet per second	
Squirrel	15 miles per hour	

Animal	Constant Speed	Common Unit Speed
Tortoise	12 inches per minute	
Hare	18.5 miles per half hour	
Raccoon	288 miles per day	
Chipmunk	1,848 feet per minute	
Fox	45.5 feet per second	
Squirrel	15 miles per hour	

Animal	Constant Speed	Common Unit Speed
Tortoise	12 inches per minute	
Hare	18.5 miles per half hour	
Raccoon	288 miles per day	
Chipmunk	1,848 feet per minute	
Fox	45.5 feet per second	
Squirrel	15 miles per hour	

TWEET CARDS

_____ on Twitter
(Your name)

I can send _____ tweets in _____ minutes.

Tweets per hour =

_____ on Twitter
(Your name)

I can send _____ tweets in _____ minutes.

Tweets per hour =

_____ on Twitter
(Your name)

I can send _____ tweets in _____ minutes.

Tweets per hour =

_____ on Twitter
(Your name)

I can send _____ tweets in _____ minutes.

Tweets per hour =

_____ on Twitter
(Your name)

I can send _____ tweets in _____ minutes.

Tweets per hour =

_____ on Twitter
(Your name)

I can send _____ tweets in _____ minutes.

Tweets per hour =

_____ on Twitter
(Your name)

I can send _____ tweets in _____ minutes.

Tweets per hour =

_____ on Twitter
(Your name)

I can send _____ tweets in _____ minutes.

Tweets per hour =

EQUAL RATIOS Xs AND Os GAME BOARD

8:7	3 to 11	32 to 4	1 to 7	1:4
15 to 10	8:12	2:3	5:30	25 to 30
8 to 20	8:1	3 to 15	21 to 15	5:3
1:6	36:18	8:10	3:12	4:5
1:10	5:6	7:5	10 to 3	2:9
4:28	20:12	5 to 6	2:5	40:35
11 to 7	3:2	20 to 24	6:3	10:100
9:33	40:12	4:18	1:5	22:14

ONLINE SHOPPING LIST

Online Shopping List			
Item	List Price	Price Adjustment	Final Price
1.			
2.			
3.			
4.			
5.			

Online Shopping List			
Item	List Price	Price Adjustment	Final Price
1.			
2.			
3.			
4.			
5.			

Online Shopping List			
Item	List Price	Price Adjustment	Final Price
1.			
2.			
3.			
4.			
5.			

PRICE ADJUSTMENT CARDS

This item is on sale. Include a 17% discount.	The final price for this item is $42.50. What percent of an adjustment is this price from the original list price?	This item is marked down by $10.00 with an additional 5% discount.
Choose any single item on your list to reduce by 10%.	This item is 25% off the original list price.	This item was reduced 20% for a sale, but the sale has ended. The reduced priced has now been increased by 15% of the sale price.
This item is reduced by $12.50. What percent decrease of the list price is this price adjustment from the original price?	This item is on sale for 15% off a 30% discounted price.	This item is marked down by $5.00 with an additional 10% discount.
There is an additional shipping fee for this item. Please add 12%.	Your discount is calculated as one-half of the difference in the original price between your two least expensive items.	This item is on sale for 30% off a 15% reduction from the original list price.

BASEBALL CARD COLLECTION NUMBER LINES

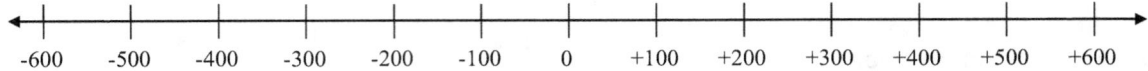

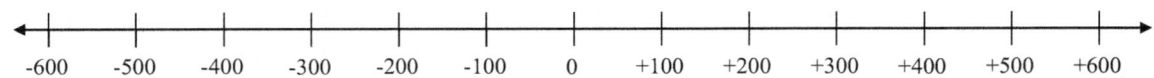

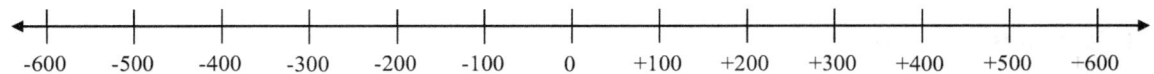

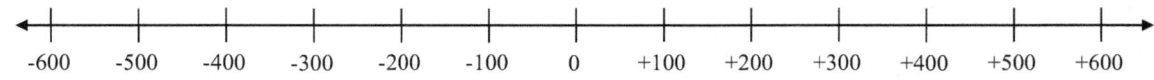

SEQUENCE CARDS A–I

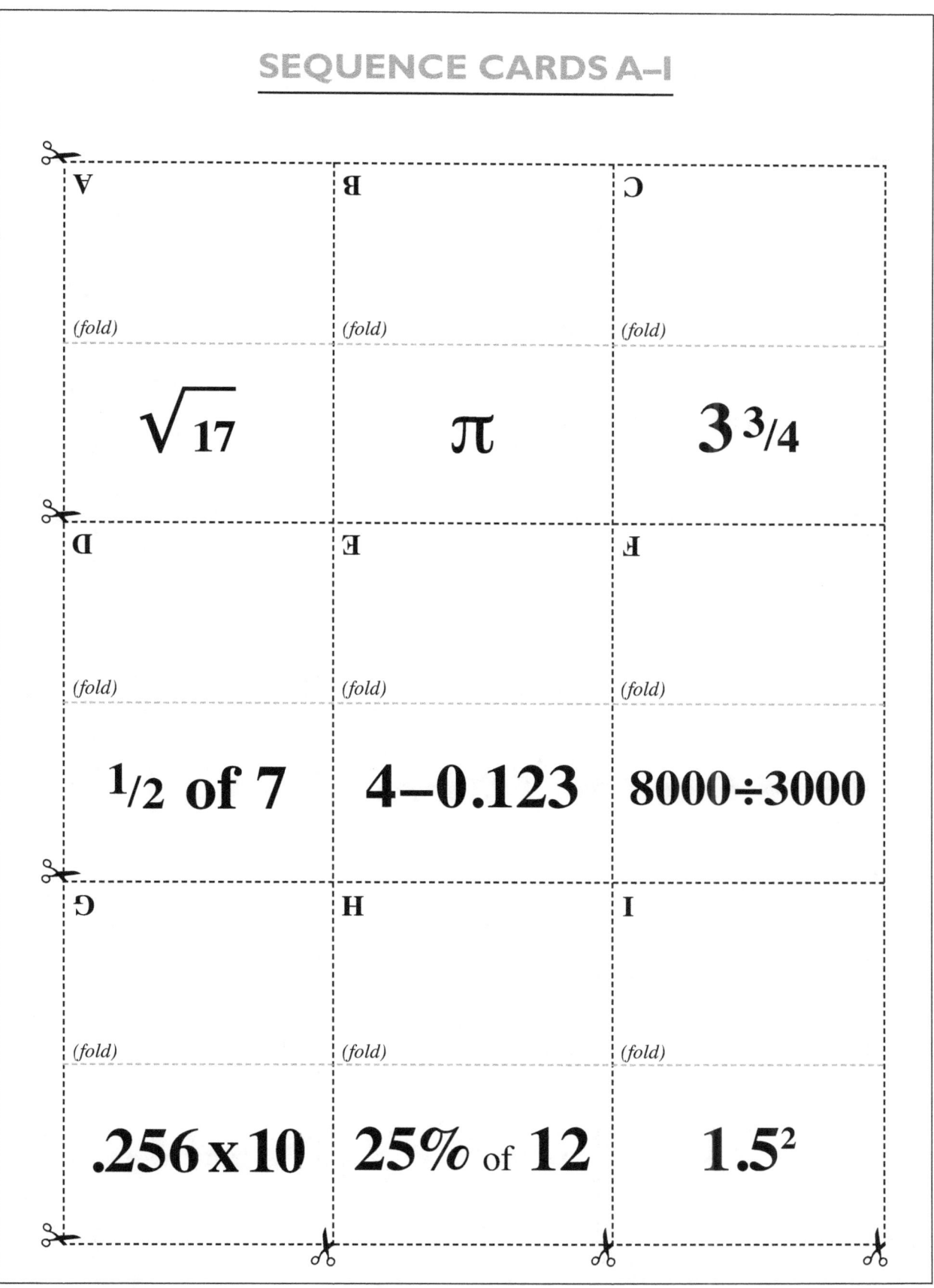

A	B	C
(fold)	(fold)	(fold)
$\sqrt{17}$	π	$3^{3/4}$

D	E	F
(fold)	(fold)	(fold)
½ of 7	4 − 0.123	8000 ÷ 3000

G	H	I
(fold)	(fold)	(fold)
.256 × 10	25% of 12	1.5^2

BLANK SEQUENCE CARDS

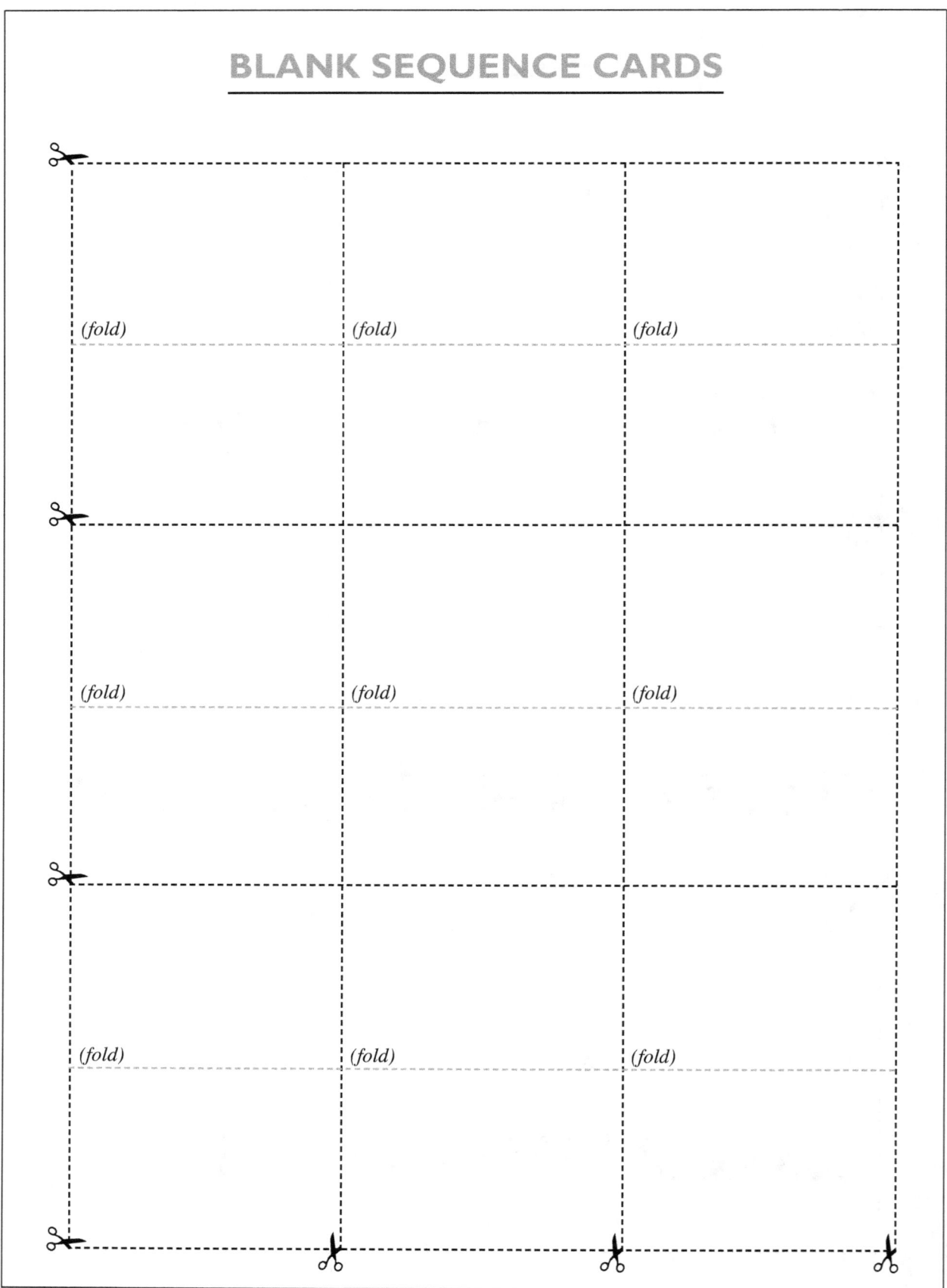

LISA'S SUB SHOP PROBLEM CARDS

A. How many $\frac{1}{3}$ servings can you get out of $\frac{1}{2}$ of a sub?
B. How many $\frac{2}{5}$ servings can you get out of $\frac{8}{10}$ of a sub?
C. How many $\frac{1}{3}$ servings can you get out of $\frac{3}{4}$ of a sub?
D. How many $\frac{1}{2}$ servings can you get out of $\frac{5}{8}$ of a sub?
E. How many $\frac{1}{3}$ servings can you get out of $\frac{8}{12}$ of a sub?
F. How many $\frac{1}{2}$ servings can you get out of $\frac{5}{7}$ of a sub?
G. How many $\frac{1}{6}$ servings can you get out of $\frac{2}{3}$ of a sub?
H. How many $\frac{1}{8}$ servings can you get out of $\frac{3}{4}$ of a sub?
I. How many $\frac{1}{4}$ servings can you get out of $\frac{3}{4}$ of a sub?
J. How many $\frac{1}{2}$ servings can you get out of $\frac{8}{12}$ of a sub?
K. How many $\frac{1}{3}$ servings can you get out of $\frac{3}{6}$ of a sub?
L. How many $\frac{2}{4}$ servings can you get out of $\frac{2}{3}$ of a sub?
M. How many $\frac{2}{4}$ servings can you get out of $\frac{8}{10}$ of a sub?
N. How many $\frac{3}{6}$ servings can you get out of $\frac{3}{4}$ of a sub?
O. How many $\frac{1}{2}$ servings can you get out of $\frac{2}{3}$ of a sub?
P. How many $\frac{1}{2}$ servings can you get out of $\frac{3}{5}$ of a sub?
Q. How many $\frac{1}{3}$ servings can you get out of $\frac{6}{9}$ of a sub?

LISA'S SUB SHOP FRACTIONS: WHOLES AND HALVES

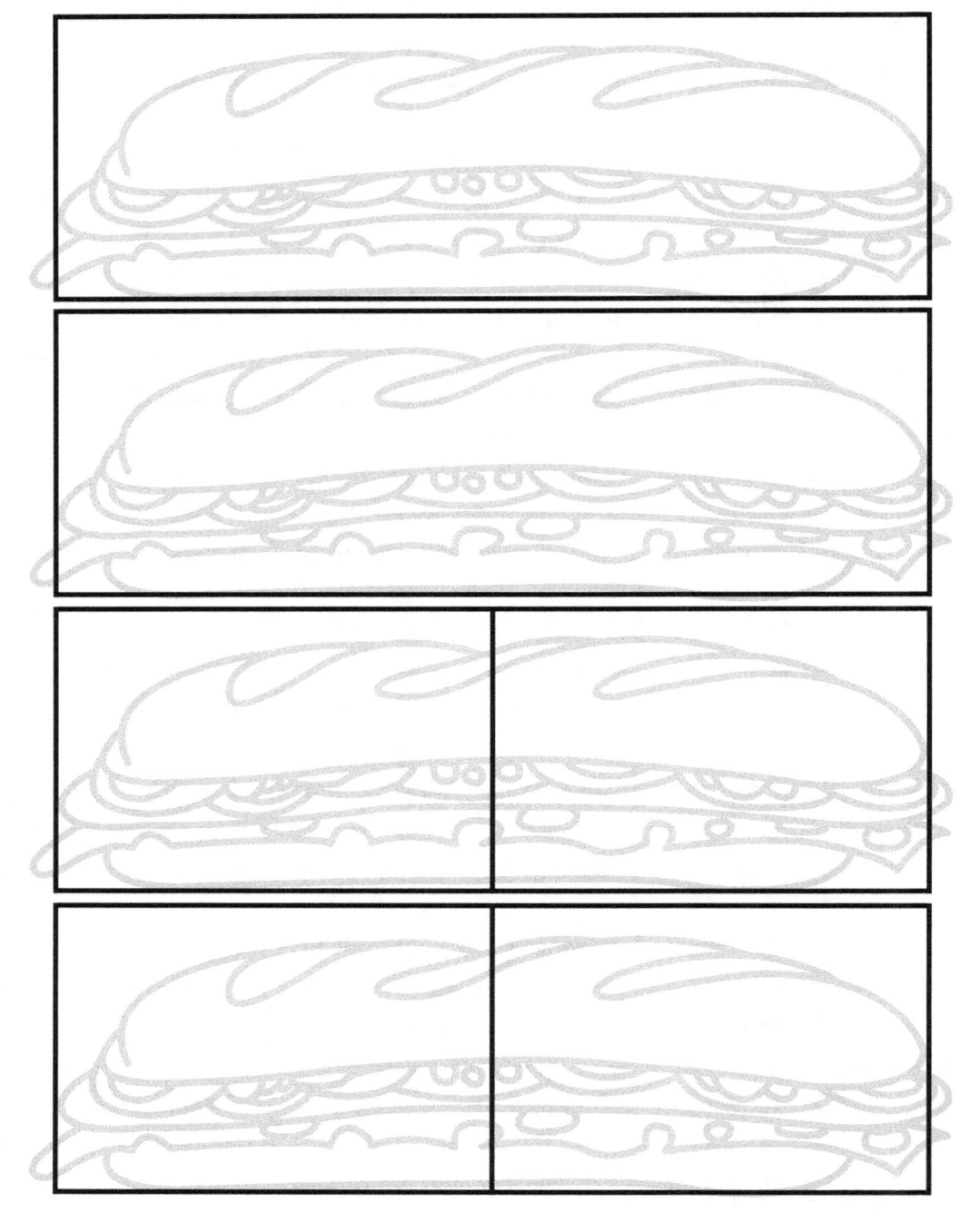

LISA'S SUB SHOP FRACTIONS: THIRDS AND FOURTHS

LISA'S SUB SHOP FRACTIONS: FIFTHS AND SIXTHS

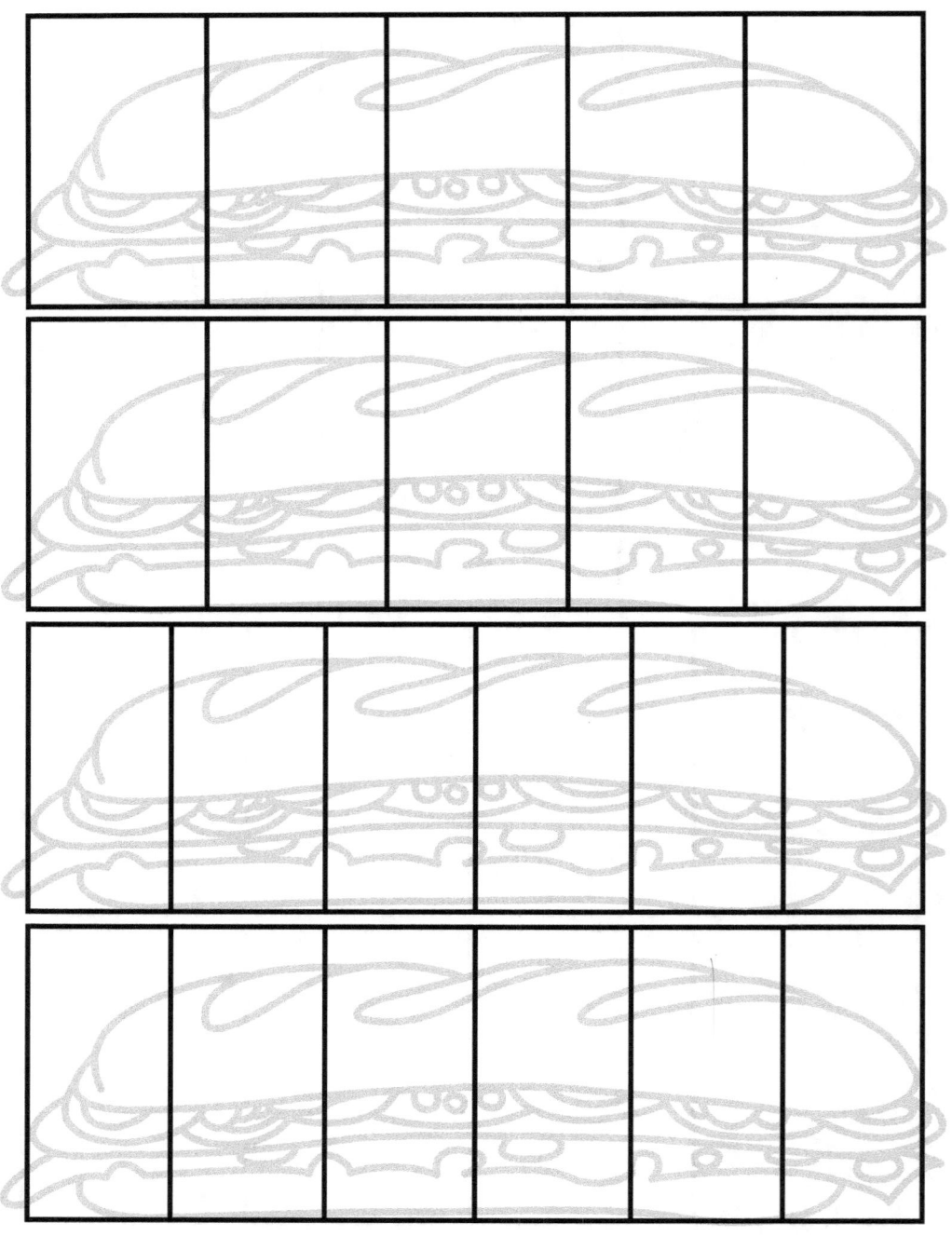

LISA'S SUB SHOP FRACTIONS: SEVENTHS AND EIGHTHS

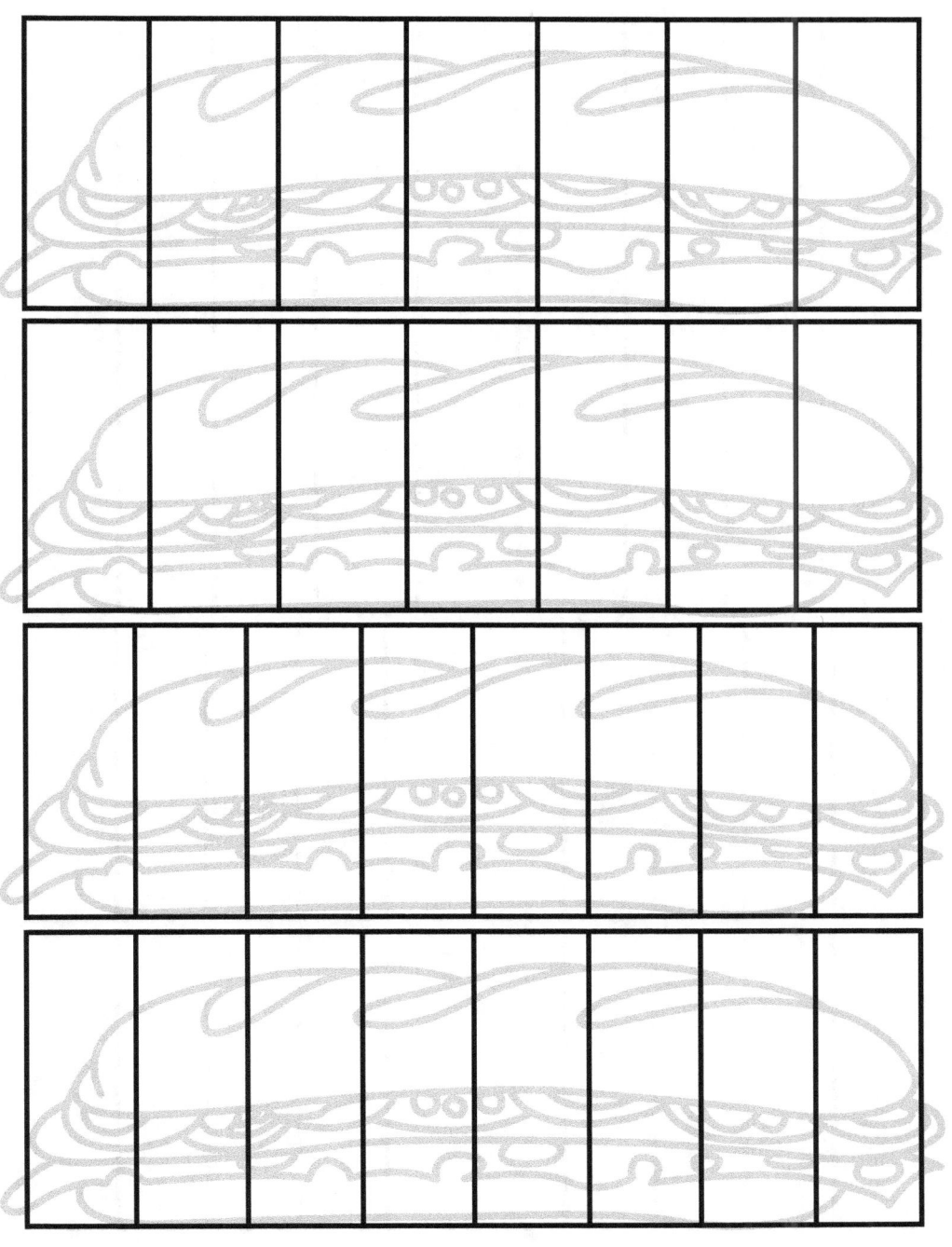

LISA'S SUB SHOP FRACTIONS: NINTHS AND TENTHS

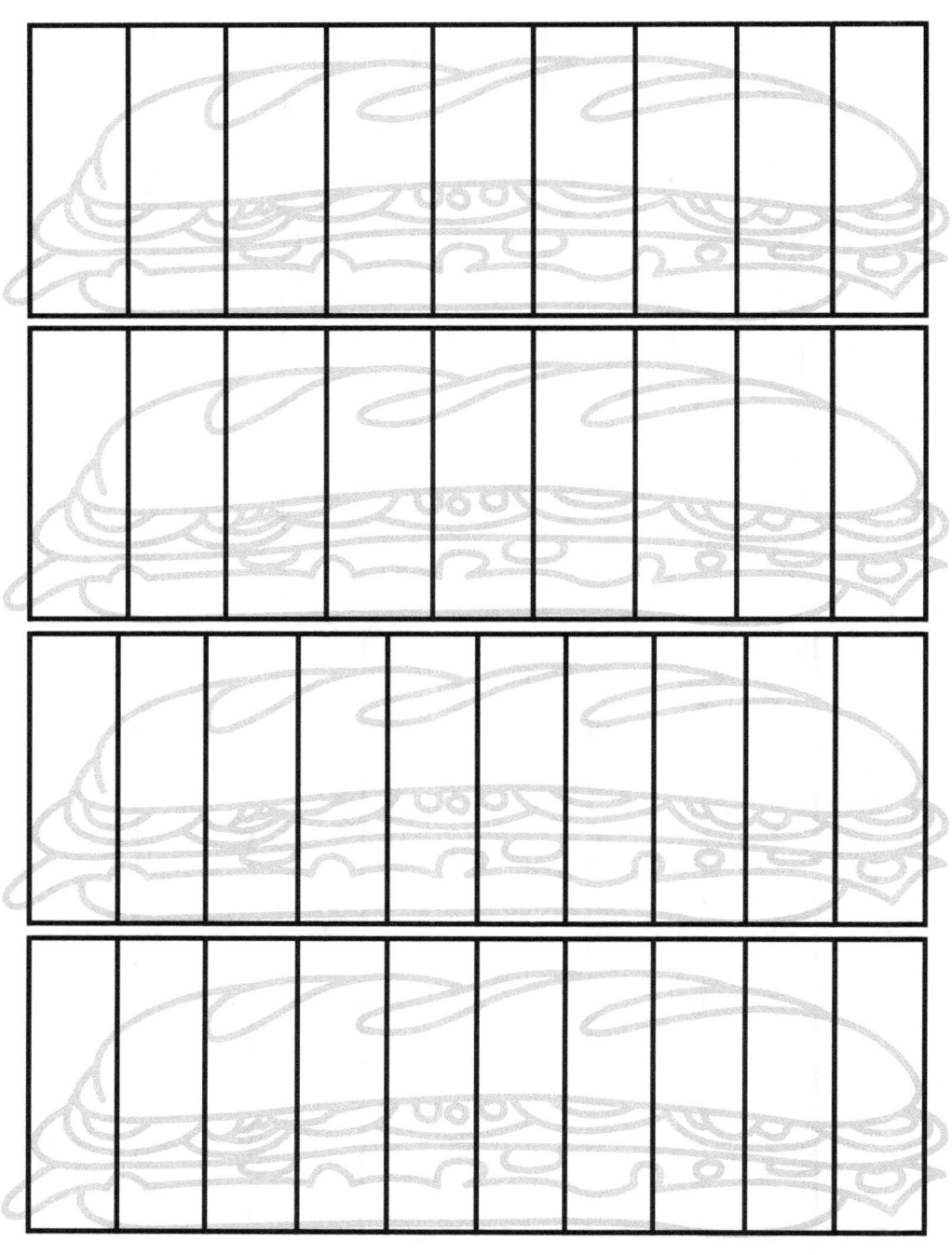

LISA'S SUB SHOP FRACTIONS: ELEVENTHS AND TWELFTHS

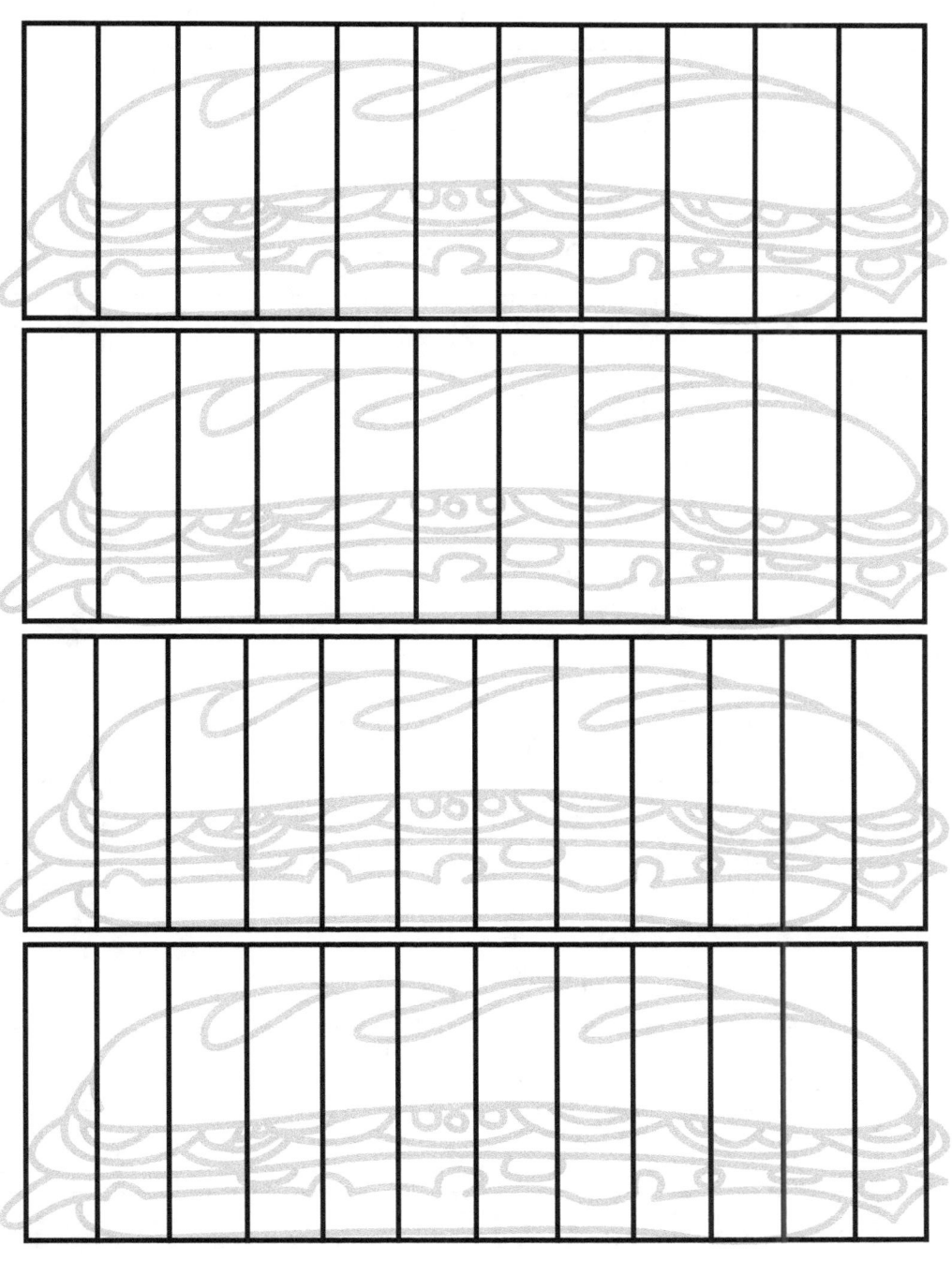

LISA'S SUB SHOP ANSWERS

A. $\frac{1}{2} \div \frac{1}{3} = 1\frac{1}{2}$
B. $\frac{8}{10} \div \frac{2}{5} = 2$
C. $\frac{3}{4} \div \frac{1}{3} = 2\frac{1}{4}$
D. $\frac{5}{8} \div \frac{1}{2} = 1\frac{1}{4}$
E. $\frac{8}{12} \div \frac{1}{3} = 2$
F. $\frac{5}{7} \div \frac{1}{2} = 1\frac{3}{7}$
G. $\frac{2}{3} \div \frac{1}{6} = 4$
H. $\frac{3}{4} \div \frac{1}{8} = 6$
I. $\frac{3}{4} \div \frac{1}{4} = 3$
J. $\frac{8}{12} \div \frac{1}{2} = 1\frac{1}{3}$
K. $\frac{3}{6} \div \frac{1}{3} = 1\frac{1}{2}$
L. $\frac{2}{3} \div \frac{2}{4} = 1\frac{1}{3}$
M. $\frac{8}{10} \div \frac{2}{4} = 1\frac{3}{5}$
N. $\frac{3}{4} \div \frac{3}{6} = 1\frac{1}{2}$
O. $\frac{2}{3} \div \frac{1}{2} = 1\frac{1}{3}$
P. $\frac{3}{5} \div \frac{1}{2} = 1\frac{1}{5}$
Q. $\frac{6}{9} \div \frac{1}{3} = 2$

FLIP CUP DECIMALS EQUATION CARDS

A. $65.30 \times \square 7.24 = 1{,}125.772$	B. $52.4 \times 16.12 = 844.68\square$
C. $258.615 = 3.1\square \times 82.1$	D. $252.5676 = 9.\square \times 27.453$
E. $10\square.615 \div 5.3 = 19.55$	F. $409.\square 68 \div 32.85 = 12.48$
G. $1\square.3 = 363.3 \div 21$	H. $\square.3 = 55.61 \div 6.7$
I. $305.1 - 9\square.59 = 210.51$	J. $41.775 - 13.\square 4 = 28.135$
K. $19.63 = 26.99 - 7.3\square$	L. $637.77 = 740.2 - 1\square 2.43$
M. $262.5 + 84.51 = 347.0\square$	N. $823.\square + 26.3 = 849.7$
O. $66.7 = 47.2 + 19.\square$	P. $78.6\square = 57.33 + 21.3$

COORDINATE TARGET

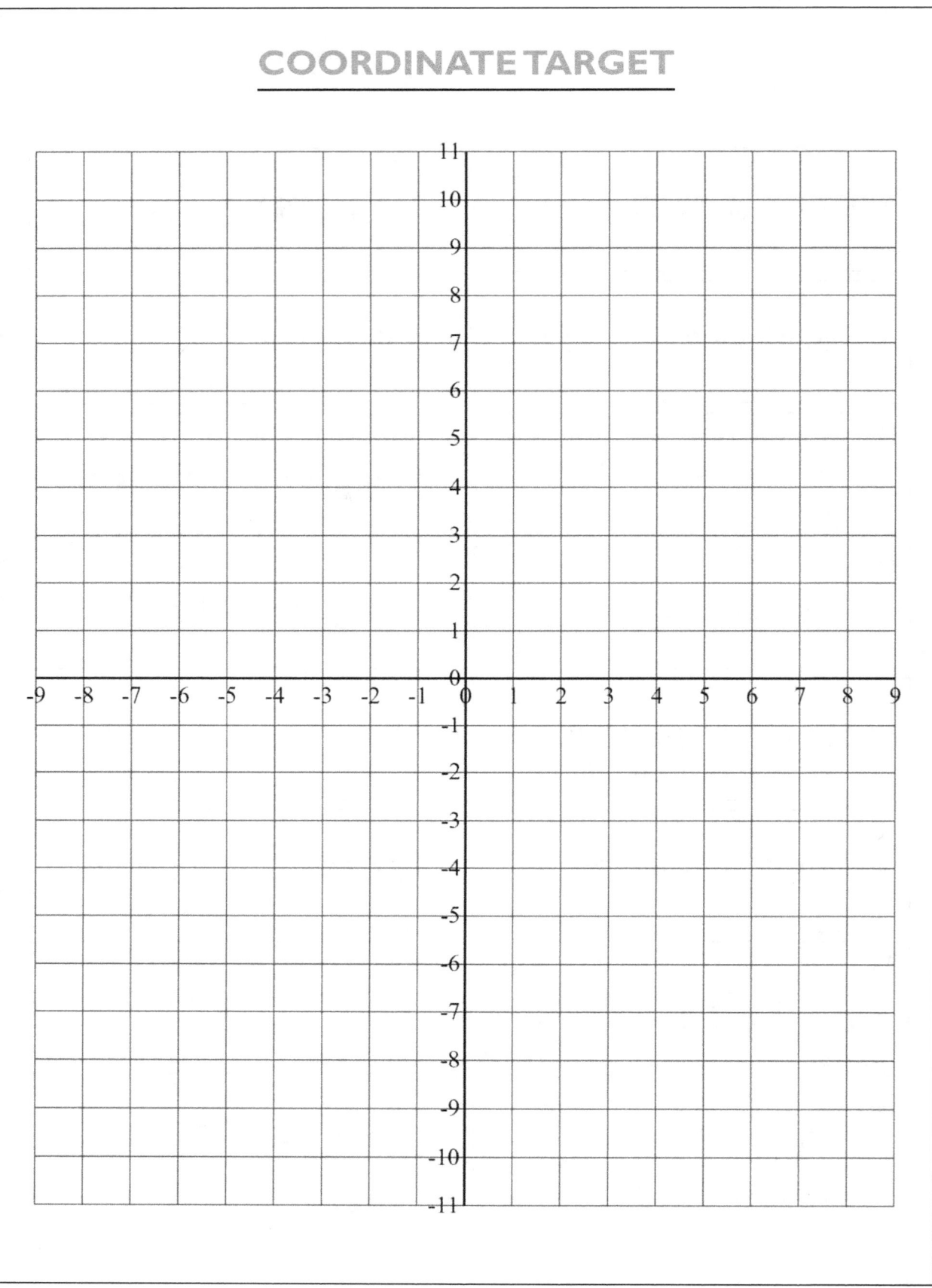

RATIONAL NUMBER CARDS

1	1	1	2	2
2	3	3	3	4
4	5	5	6	6
−1	−1	−1	−2	−2
−2	−3	−3	−3	−4
−4	−5	−5	−6	−6

NUMBER LINE MOUNTAIN

TUMBLE TOWER EQUIVALENT EXPRESSIONS RECORDING SHEET

	Initial Expression	Distributed	Simplified
A		$(5 \cdot y) + (5 \cdot 2)$	$5y + 10$
B	$7(-7y-5)$		$-49y - 35$
C	$2(-4 + 8y)$	$(2 \cdot -4) + (2 \cdot 8y)$	
D		$(2 \cdot 5y) + (2 \cdot 5)$	$10y + 10$
E	$-3(y + 4)$		$-3y - 12$
F	$(-5 + y)3$	$(-5 \cdot 3) + (y \cdot 3)$	
G		$(3 \cdot 7y) + (3 \cdot 2)$	$21y + 6$
H	$4(2y - 3)$		$8y - 12$
I	$2(5y + 3)$	$(2 \cdot 5y) + (2 \cdot 3)$	
J		$(3 \cdot 3y) - (3 \cdot 3)$	$9y - 9$
K	$5(2y + 3)$		$10y + 15$
L	$4(5 + 2y)$	$(4 \cdot 5) + (4 \cdot 2y)$	
M		$(2 \cdot x) + (2 \cdot 12)$	$2x + 24$
N	$2(3y + 5)$		$6y + 10$
O	$6(3y - 5) - 2(10 + 4y)$	$(6 \cdot 3y) - (6 \cdot 5) - (2 \cdot 10) - (2 \cdot 4y)$	
P	$2(y + 5) + 2(3 + y)$		$16 + 4y$
Q	$6(1 + y) - 3y(-2 + 4y)$		$6 + 12y - 12y^2$
R	$3(2y + 5)$	$(3 \cdot 2y) + (3 \cdot 5)$	
S		$(6 \cdot 2y) - (6 \cdot 3)$	$12y - 18$
T	$2(3y + 5)$		$6y + 10$
U	$4(2y + 5y)$	$(4 \cdot 2y) + (4 \cdot 5y)$	
V		$(6 \cdot 4) + (6 \cdot 2y)$	$24 + 12y$
W	$5(3y + 2y)$		$25y$
X	$3(3y + 4)$	$(3 \cdot 3y) + (3 \cdot 4)$	
Y		$(-2 \cdot 3y) + (-2 \cdot 2)$	$-6y - 4$
Z	$9(2y + 3)$		$18y + 27$
AA	$4(10 + 5y)$	$(4 \cdot 10) + (4 \cdot 5y)$	

TUMBLE TOWER ANSWERS

	Initial Expression	Distributed	Simplified
A	5(y + 2)	(5 • y) + (5 • 2)	5y + 10
B	7(−7y − 5)	(7 • −7y) − (7 • 5)	−49y − 35
C	2(−4 + 8y)	(2 • −4) + (2 • 8y)	−8 + 16y
D	2(5y + 5)	(2 • 5y) + (2 • 5)	10y + 10
E	−3(y + 4)	(−3 • y) + (3 • 4)	−3y − 12
F	(−5 + y)3	(−5 • 3) + (y • 3)	−15 + 3y
G	3(7y + 2)	(3 • 7y) + (3 • 2)	21y + 6
H	4(2y − 3)	(4 • 2y) − (3 • 4)	8y − 12
I	2(5y + 3)	(2 • 5y) + (2 • 3)	10y + 6
J	3(3y − 3)	(3 • 3y) − (3 • 3)	9y − 9
K	5(2y + 3)	(5 • 2y) + (5 • 3)	10y + 15
L	4(5 + 2y)	(4 • 5) + (4 • 2y)	20 + 8y
M	2(x + 12)	(2 • x) + (2 • 12)	2x + 24
N	2(3y + 5)	(2 • 3y) + (2 • 5)	6y + 10
O	6(3y − 5) − 2(10 + 4y)	(6 • 3y) − (6 • 5) − (2 • 10) − (2 • 4y)	10y − 50
P	2(y + 5) + 2(3 + y)	(2y + 10) + (6 + 2y)	16 + 4y
Q	6(1 + y) − 3y(−2 + 4y)	(6 • 1) + 6y + (3y • 2) − (3y • 4y)	$6 + 12y − 12y^2$
R	3(2y + 5)	(3 • 2y) + (3 • 5)	6y + 15
S	6(2y − 3)	(6 • 2y) − (6 • 3)	12y − 18
T	2(3y + 5)	(2 • 3y) + (2 • 5)	6y + 10
U	4(2y + 5y)	(4 • 2y) + (4 • 5y)	28y
V	6(4 + 2y)	(6 • 4) + (6 • 2y)	24 + 12y
W	5(3y + 2y)	(5 • 3y) + (5 • 2y)	25y
X	3(3y + 4)	(3 • 3y) + (3 • 4)	9y + 12
Y	−2(3y + 2)	(−2 • 3y) + (−2 • 2)	−6y − 4
Z	9(2y + 3)	(9 • 2y) + (9 • 3)	18y + 27
AA	4(10 + 5y)	(4 • 10) + (4 • 5y)	40 + 20y

JEANS AND SHIRTS GAME BOARD

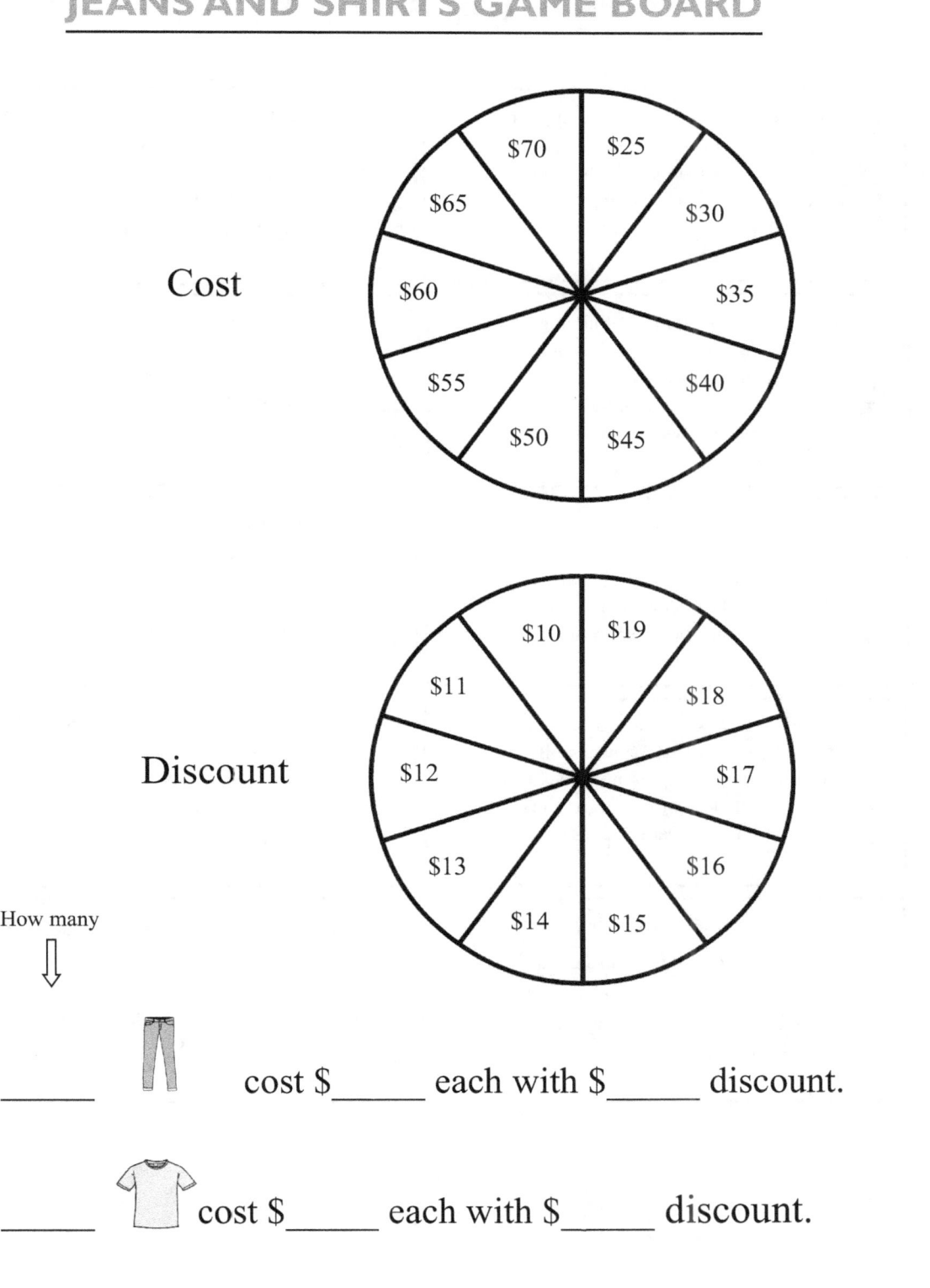

How many ⬇

_____ 👖 cost $_____ each with $_____ discount.

_____ 👕 cost $_____ each with $_____ discount.

BURNING CANDLES PROBLEM CARDS

a. A candle is 12 inches tall after burning for 1 hour. After 3 hours it is 8 inches tall. Create a table to represent the height y of the candle after burning x hours. Graph the linear relationship.

b. A candle is 12 inches tall after burning for 2 hours. After 6 hours it is 6 inches tall. Create a table to represent the height y of the candle after burning x hours. Graph the linear relationship.

c. A candle is 5½ inches tall after burning for 2 hours. After 5 hours it is 4 inches tall. Create a table to represent the height y of the candle after burning x hours. Graph the linear relationship.

d. A candle is 9 inches tall after burning for 2 hours. After 4 hours it is 6 inches tall. Create a table to represent the height y of the candle after burning x hours. Graph the linear relationship.

e. A candle is 2 inches tall after burning for 1 hour. After 5 hours it is 1 inch tall. Create a table to represent the height y of the candle after burning x hours. Graph the linear relationship.

f. A candle is 5 inches tall after burning for 1 hour. After 7 hours it is 2 inches tall. Create a table to represent the height y of the candle after burning x hours. Graph the linear relationship.

g. A candle is 4 inches tall after burning for 2 hours. After 4 hours it is 2 inches tall. Create a table to represent the height y of the candle after burning x hours. Graph the linear relationship.

h. A candle is 9 inches tall after burning for 3 hours. After 8 hours it is 4 inches tall. Create a table to represent the height y of the candle after burning x hours. Graph the linear relationship.

i. A candle is $10\frac{1}{2}$ inches tall after burning for 3 hours. After 7 hours it is $4\frac{1}{2}$ inches tall. Create a table to represent the height y of the candle after burning x hours. Graph the linear relationship.

j. A candle is 10 inches tall after burning for 4 hours. After 7 hours it is 4 inches tall. Create a table to represent the height y of the candle after burning x hours. Graph the linear relationship.

BURNING CANDLES ANSWERS

Inches	14	12	10	8	6	4	2	0
Hours	0	1	2	3	4	5	6	7

Inches	15	$13\frac{1}{2}$	12	$10\frac{1}{2}$	9	$7\frac{1}{2}$	6	$4\frac{1}{2}$	3	$1\frac{1}{2}$	0
Hours	0	1	2	3	4	5	6	7	8	9	10

Inches	$6\frac{1}{2}$	6	$5\frac{1}{2}$	5	$4\frac{1}{2}$	4	$3\frac{1}{2}$	3	$2\frac{1}{2}$	2	$1\frac{1}{2}$	1	$\frac{1}{2}$	0
Hours	0	1	2	3	4	5	6	7	8	9	10	11	12	13

Inches	12	$10\frac{1}{2}$	9	$7\frac{1}{2}$	6	$4\frac{1}{2}$	3	$1\frac{1}{2}$	0
Hours	0	1	2	3	4	5	6	7	8

Inches	$2\frac{1}{4}$	2	$1\frac{3}{4}$	$1\frac{1}{2}$	$1\frac{1}{4}$	1	$\frac{3}{4}$	$\frac{1}{2}$	$\frac{1}{4}$	0
Hours	0	1	2	3	4	5	6	7	8	9

Inches	$5\frac{1}{2}$	5	$4\frac{1}{2}$	4	$3\frac{1}{2}$	3	$2\frac{1}{2}$	2	$1\frac{1}{2}$	1	$\frac{1}{2}$	0
Hours	0	1	2	3	4	5	6	7	8	9	10	11

Inches	6	5	4	3	2	1	0
Hours	0	1	2	3	4	5	6

Inches	12	11	10	9	8	7	6	5	4	3	2	1	0
Hours	0	1	2	3	4	5	6	7	8	9	10	11	12

Inches	15	$13\frac{1}{2}$	12	$10\frac{1}{2}$	9	$7\frac{1}{2}$	6	$4\frac{1}{2}$	3	$1\frac{1}{2}$	0
Hours	0	1	2	3	4	5	6	7	8	9	10

Inches	18	16	14	12	10	8	6	4	2	0
Hours	0	1	2	3	4	5	6	7	8	9

SHOOT FOR THE TRUTH INEQUITY CARDS

97 ☐ 9.7 × 10^2	30 ☐ 0.3 × 10^1
338 ☐ 3.38 × 10^2	97 ☐ 9.7 × 10^2
660 ☐ 6.6 × 10^2	35 ☐ 3.5 × 10^3
5,450 ☐ 5.45 × 10^2	1,000 ☐ 10 × 10^3
233.8 ☐ 2.338 × 10^3	10,000 ☐ 10 × 10^3
9,070 ☐ 9.07 × 10^2	67,500 ☐ 6.75 × 10^3
0.5 ☐ 0.5 × 10^1	619 ☐ 6.19 × 10^2
34.7 ☐ 3.47 × 10^2	540 ☐ 5.4 × 10^2
4,800 ☐ 4.8 × 10^2	260 ☐ 2.6 × 10^3
1,220 ☐ 1.22 × 10^3	8.7 ☐ 8.7 × 10^1
231 ☐ 2.31 × 10^3	930 ☐ 9.3 × 10^2
200 ☐ 0.2 × 10^2	86 ☐ 8.6 × 10^1
97 ☐ 9.7 × 10^0	44,300 ☐ 4.43 × 10^3
10 ☐ 0.01 × 10^2	236.9 ☐ 2.369 × 10^3
2,220 ☐ .222 × 10^3	9,600 ☐ 0.96 × 10^3
1,110 ☐ 0.111 × 10^4	6,969 ☐ 69.69 × 10^3
883 ☐ .883 × 10^2	10 ☐ 0.01 × 10^2
1,234 ☐ .1234 × 10^3	3 ☐ 0.003 × 10^3
4.156 ☐ 4.156 × 10^0	10,101 ☐ 1.0101 × 10^4
555.0 ☐ 55.5 × 10^1	660.6 ☐ 66.06 × 10^2

SHOOT FOR THE TRUTH INEQUITY CARDS ANSWERS

$97 < 9.7 \times 10^2$	$30 > 0.3 \times 10^1$
$338 = 3.38 \times 10^2$	$97 < 9.7 \times 10^2$
$660 = 6.6 \times 10^2$	$35 < 3.5 \times 10^3$
$5{,}450 > 5.45 \times 10^2$	$1{,}000 < 10 \times 10^3$
$233.8 < 2.338 \times 10^3$	$10{,}000 = 10 \times 10^3$
$9{,}070 > 9.07 \times 10^2$	$67{,}500 > 6.75 \times 10^3$
$0.5 < 0.5 \times 10^1$	$619 = 6.19 \times 10^2$
$34.7 < 3.47 \times 10^2$	$540 = 5.4 \times 10^2$
$4{,}800 > 4.8 \times 10^2$	$260 < 2.6 \times 10^3$
$1{,}220 = 1.22 \times 10^3$	$8.7 < 8.7 \times 10^1$
$231 < 2.31 \times 10^3$	$930 = 9.3 \times 10^2$
$200 > 0.2 \times 10^2$	$86 = 8.6 \times 10^1$
$97 > 9.7 \times 10^0$	$44{,}300 > 4.43 \times 10^3$
$10 > 0.01 \times 10^2$	$236.9 < 2.369 \times 10^3$
$2{,}220 > .222 \times 10^3$	$9{,}600 > 0.96 \times 10^3$
$1{,}110 = 0.111 \times 10^4$	$6{,}969 < 69.69 \times 10^3$
$883 > .883 \times 10^2$	$10 > 0.01 \times 10^2$
$1{,}234 > .1234 \times 10^3$	$3 = 0.003 \times 10^3$
$4.156 = 4.156 \times 10^0$	$10{,}101 = 1.0101 \times 10^4$
$555.0 = 55.5 \times 10^1$	$660.6 < 66.06 \times 10^2$

HIGH/LOW VALUE CARDS

12^1	15^2	30^2
7^3	9^3	4^3
3^4	6^4	10^4
1^6	4^4	5^4
8^0	$\sqrt{9}$	$\sqrt{25}$
$\sqrt{144}$	$\sqrt{400}$	$\sqrt{64}$
$\sqrt{169}$	$\sqrt{100}$	$\sqrt{625}$
$\sqrt[3]{125}$	$\sqrt[3]{729}$	$\sqrt[3]{216}$
$\sqrt[3]{512}$	$\sqrt[3]{343}$	$\sqrt[3]{1000}$
$\sqrt[4]{81}$	$\sqrt[4]{1}$	$\sqrt[5]{32}$
$.2 \times 10^3$	$.007 \times 10^4$	$.030 \times 10^5$
4.5×10^1	3×10^2	452×10^0
$.032 \times 10^3$	9.8×10^2	$.267 \times 10^2$
$1^3 \times 4^2$	$4^3 - 2^2$	$(4^2)^2$
$2^3 \times 2^2$	$(2 \times 3)^2$	$(2^2)^3$
$3^7 \div 3^4$	$2^8 \div 2^3$	$4^3 - 7^2$

PARTY WITH PENTOMINOES ANSWERS

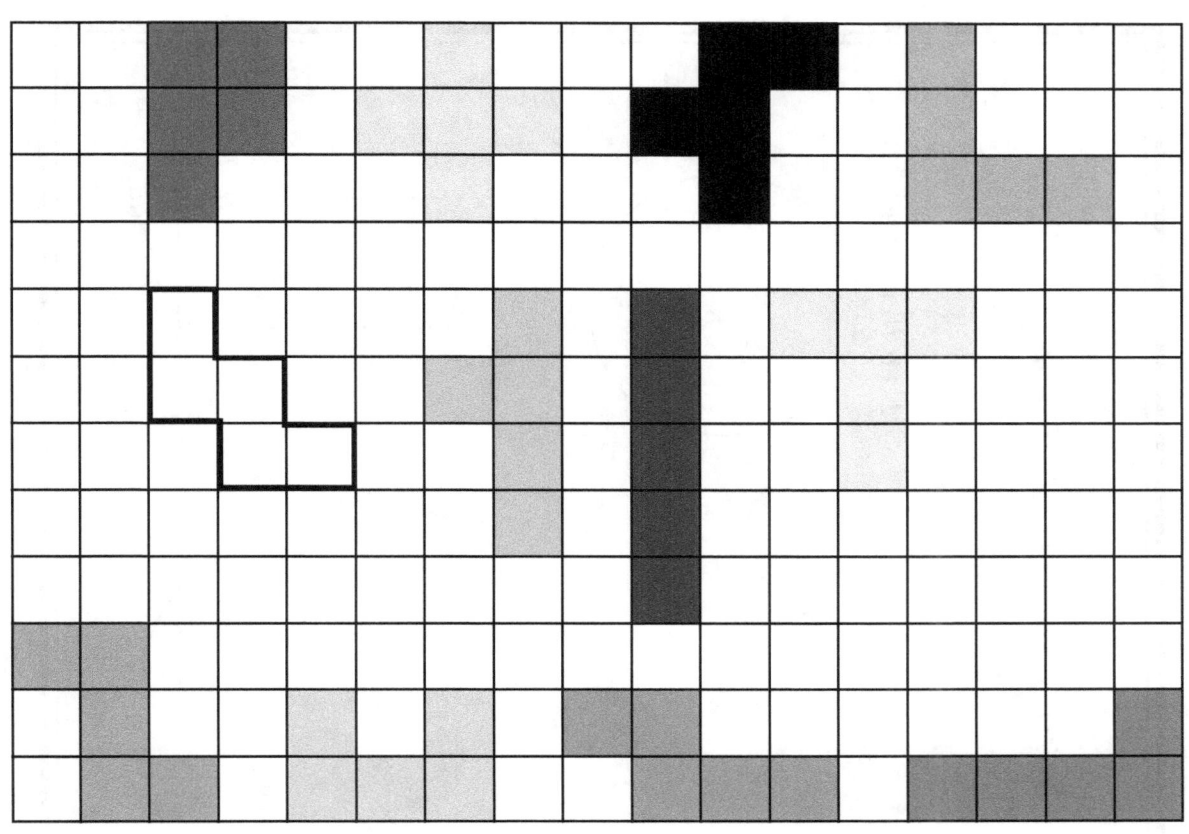
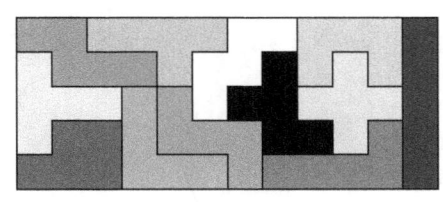
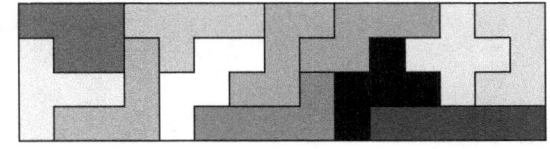

CHANCE FOR FREEBIES PLACE MAT

Thank You for Visiting our Restaurant

Free Beverage

Free Salad

Free Meal

Free Dessert

Find the probability of winning each item.

What is the probability of winning anything?

CHANCE FOR FREEBIES CHALLENGE MAT

Thank You for Visiting our Restaurant!

Design a mat with approximately a 30% chance of winning a free menu item. Show your thinking with words, symbols, and/or equations.

TRIANGLE COUSINS GAME BOARD

Triangle	Interior Angles		Sum of the Interior Angles
Equilateral	60°		180°
Scalene	60°		180°
Isosceles	55°		180°
Right	60°		180°
Acute	70°		180°
Obtuse	95°		180°

TRIANGLE COUSINS SPINNER

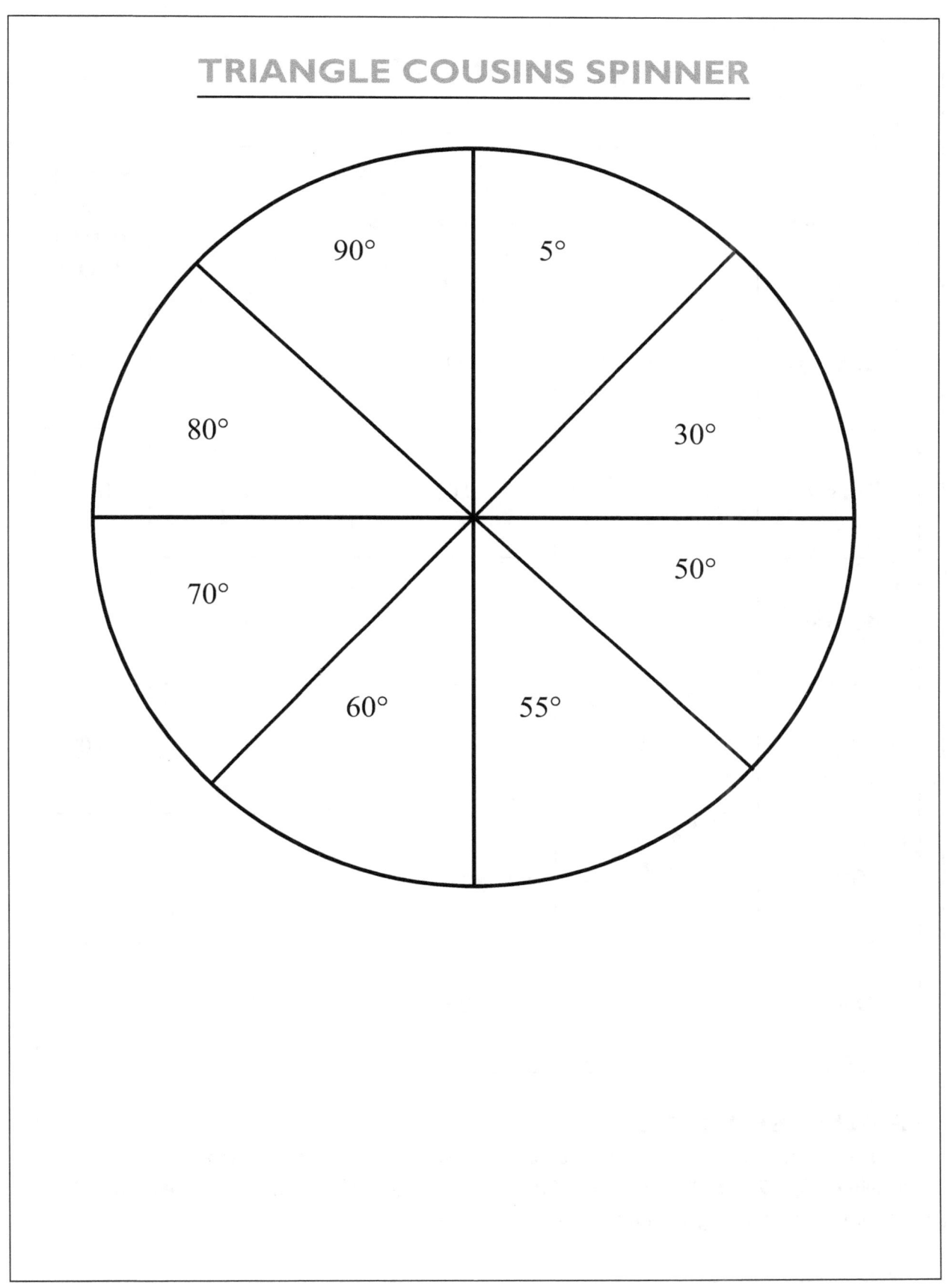

TRIANGLE COUSINS ANSWERS

Triangle	Interior Angles			Sum of the Interior Angles
Equilateral	60°	60°	60°	180°
Scalene	60°	50°	70°	180°
Isosceles	55°	70°	55°	180°
Right	60°	30°	90°	180°
Acute	70°	90°	20°	180°
Obtuse	95°	80°	5°	180°

CHALLENGE ANSWERS

The sum of the interior angles of a rectangle is twice the sum of the interior angles of a triangle (180° • 2 = 360°). The sum of the interior angles of a pentagon is three times the sum of the interior angles of a triangle (180° • 3 = 540°).

SIGMUND TRANSFORMATIONS FACES

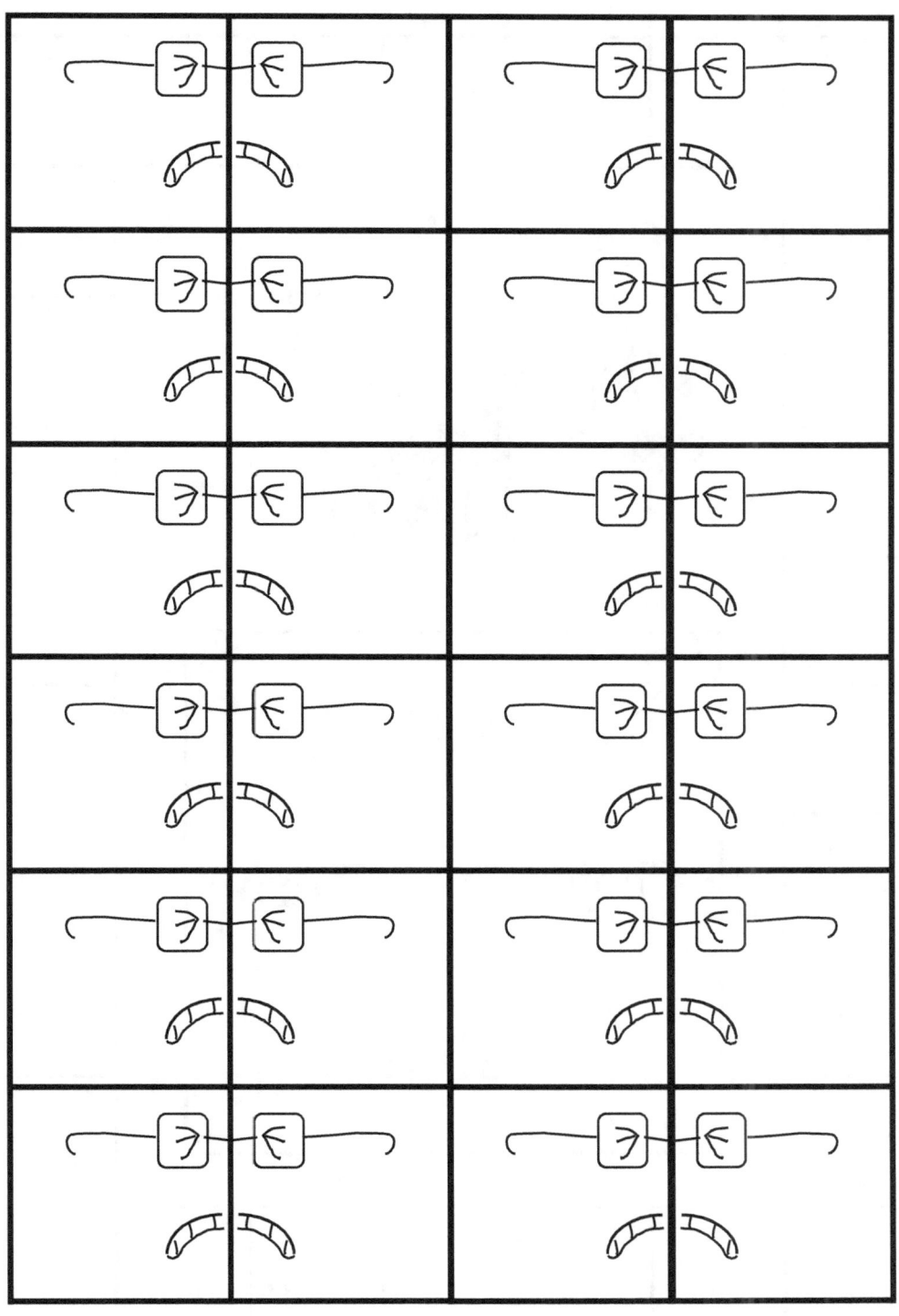

SIGMUND TRANSFORMATIONS GAME BOARD

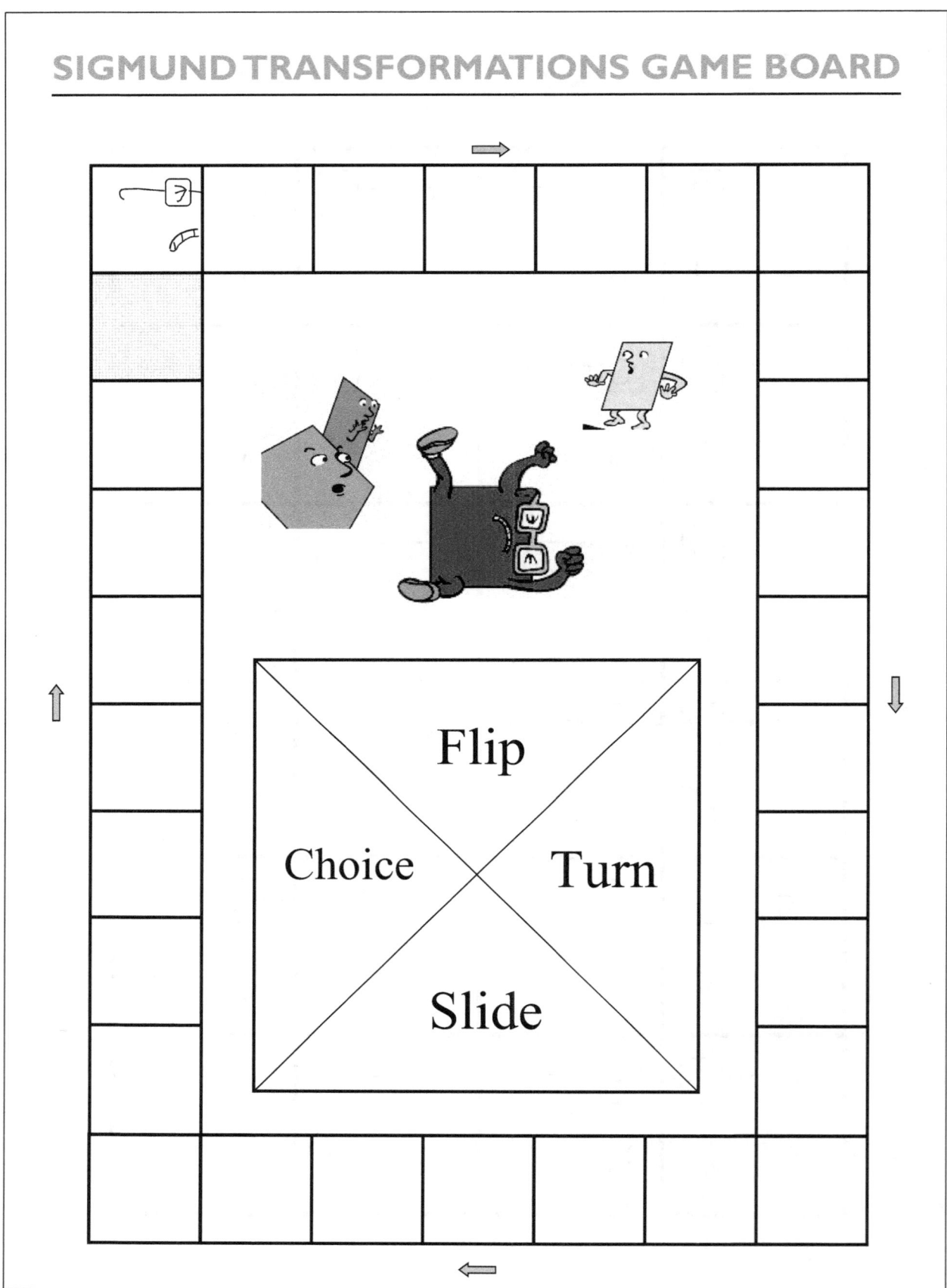

SIGMUND TRANSFORMATIONS KEY

Flip

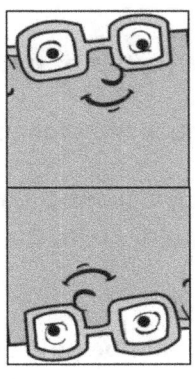 

Slide

Turn

 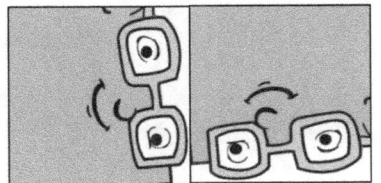

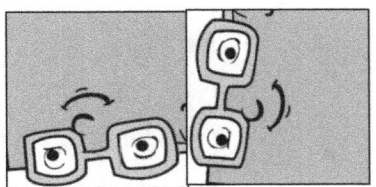 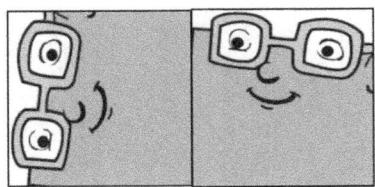

DEEP-SEA DIVING MEASURES OF CENTER

Mean, median, and mode are all measures of center (types of averages).

Mean: The sum of a set of numbers divided by the number of numbers in the set.

Median: The middle number of a set of numbers when the numbers are arranged from least to greatest (or greatest to least). If there are two numbers in the middle, use the mean of the two numbers to express the median.

Mode: The number that is the most frequent in a set of numbers. In any given set of data, there can be one mode, more than one mode, or no mode at all.

Range: The difference between the greatest number and the least number in a set of numbers.

LITERATURE STATS INFERENCE CARDS

Literature Title: Median Number of Words Per Line: Mean Number of Lines Per Page: Average Word Length:	Literature Title: Median Number of Words Per Line: Mean Number of Lines Per Page: Average Word Length:
Literature Title: Median Number of Words Per Line: Mean Number of Lines Per Page: Average Word Length:	Literature Title: Median Number of Words Per Line: Mean Number of Lines Per Page: Average Word Length:

THE PLOT THICKENS REFERENCE SHEET

Data Set

Age of Participants in 5K							
16	30	25	17	41	17	39	17
23	27	18	19	26	40	30	25
30	25	18	25	19	29	18	16
41	29	17	33	28	18	21	16

Dot Plot—a set of data displayed over a number line to show the frequency of each value

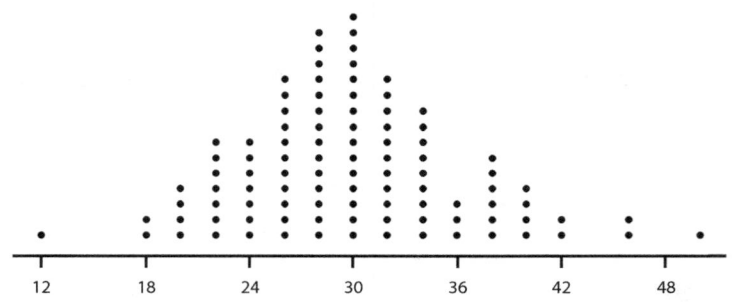

Histogram—similar to a bar graph using rectangles to show the frequency of data, except the data are grouped into equal ranges.

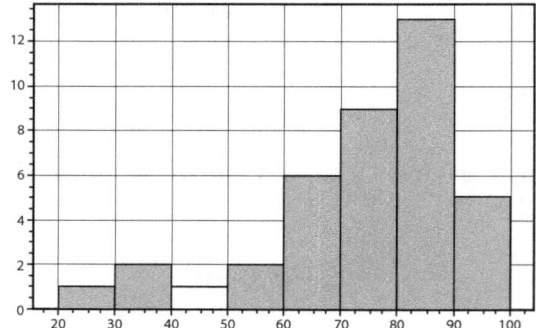

Box Plot—a graphical display based on the minimum, first quartile, median, third quartile, and maximum value of the data.

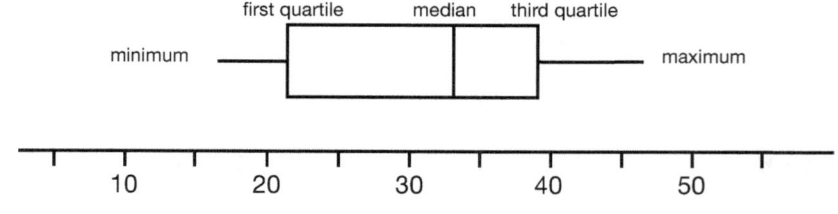

TEXTING TWEENS PROBLEMS

A. What percent of 7th grade students sent 500 texts or less?
B. What is the median number of texts that 6th grade students sent?
C. What is the range of texts sent by 7th grade students?
D. Which grade level had the highest upper quartile?
E. Which grade level had the smallest range?
F. What percent of 6th grade students sent 800 texts or less?
G. The median number of texts was 600 for which grade level/s?
H. What is the minimum value?
I. What percent of 8th grade students sent between 500 and 600 texts?
J. What was the value of the upper quartile for 8th grade students?
K. Which grade level had the lowest median?
L. What percent of the 7th grade students sent between 300 and 800 messages?
M. Which grade level had the greatest range in texts sent?
N. What percent of 6th grade students sent 600 or more texts?

TEXTING TWEENS ANSWERS

A. What percent of 7th grade students sent 500 texts or less?	50%
B. What is the median number of texts that 6th grade students sent?	600
C. What is the range of texts sent by 7th grade students?	700
D. Which grade level had the highest upper quartile?	6th
E. Which grade level had the smallest range?	8th
F. What percent of 6th grade students sent 800 texts or less?	75%
G. The median number of texts was 600 for which grade level/s?	6th and 8th
H. What is the minimum value?	100
I. What percent of 8th grade students sent between 500 and 600 texts?	25%
J. What was the value of the upper quartile for 8th grade students?	700
K. Which grade level had the lowest median?	7th
L. What percent of the 7th grade students sent between 300 and 800 messages?	75%
M. Which grade level had the greatest range in texts sent?	6th
N. What percent of 6th grade students sent 600 or more texts?	50%

FINGERPRINT TYPES CHART

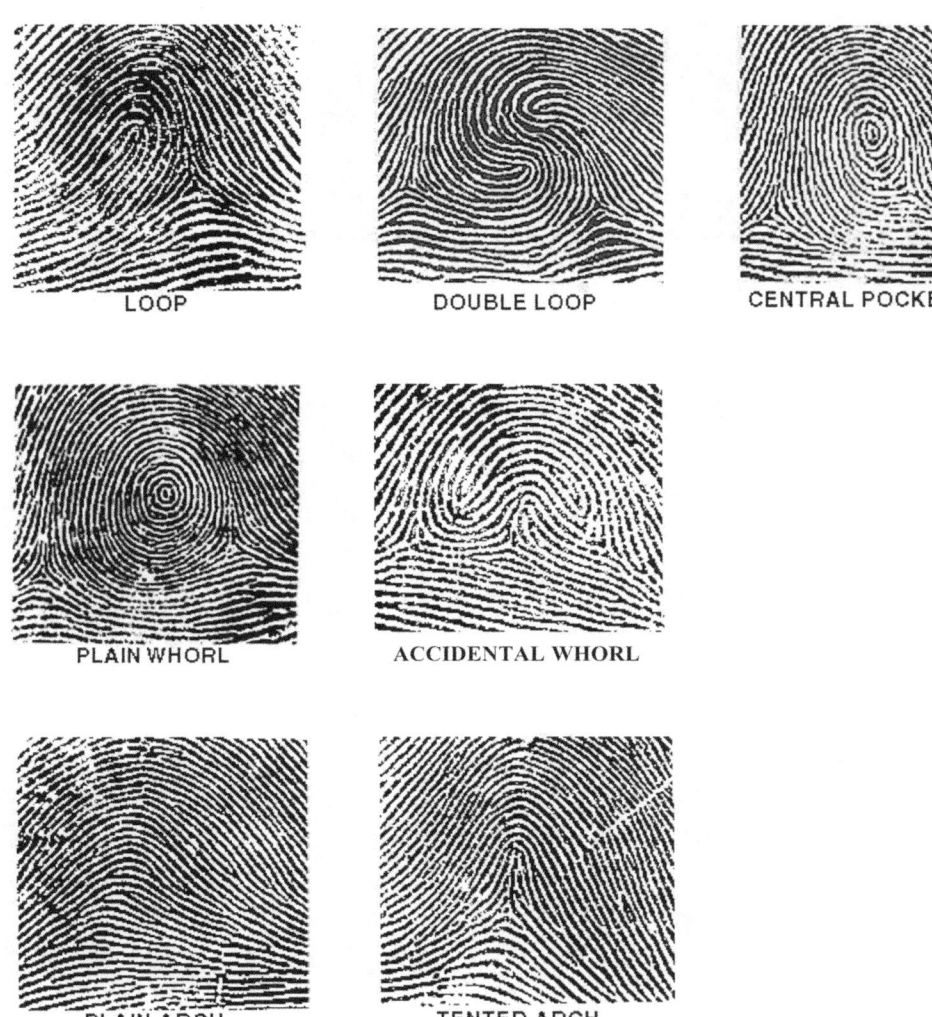

For Product Safety Concerns and Information please contact our EU representative GPSR@taylorandfrancis.com
Taylor & Francis Verlag GmbH, Kaufingerstraße 24, 80331 München, Germany

www.ingramcontent.com/pod-product-compliance
Lightning Source LLC
Chambersburg PA
CBHW081827230426
43668CB00017B/2401